# TOOLS FOR
# MATCHING READERS
# TO TEXTS

# SOLVING PROBLEMS IN THE TEACHING OF LITERACY
Cathy Collins Block, *Series Editor*

# Tools for Matching Readers to Texts

## Research-Based Practices

Heidi Anne E. Mesmer

**THE GUILFORD PRESS**
New York    London

© 2008 The Guilford Press
A Division of Guilford Publications, Inc.
72 Spring Street, New York, NY 10012
www.guilford.com

Printed in the United States of America

This book is printed on acid-free paper.

Last digit is print number:  9  8  7  6  5  4  3  2  1

Library of Congress Cataloging-in-Publication Data

Mesmer, Heidi Anne E.
    Tools for matching readers to texts : research-based practices / Heidi Anne E.
Mesmer.
        p. cm. — (Solving problems in the teaching of literacy)
    Includes bibliographical references and index.
    ISBN-13: 978-1-59385-597-0 (pbk. : alk. paper)
    ISBN-10: 1-59385-597-4 (pbk. : alk. paper)
    ISBN-13: 978-1-59385-598-7 (hardcover : alk. paper)
    ISBN-10: 1-59385-598-2 (hardcover : alk. paper)
    1. Reading (Elementary)—United States.  2. Children—Books and reading—
United States.  3. Book selection—United States.  I. Title.
    LB1573.M452 2008
    372.41—dc22
                                                          2007037699

*For my father, John, and my grandfather, Murray*

# About the Author

**Heidi Anne E. Mesmer, PhD,** is Assistant Professor at Virginia Polytechnic Institute and State University, where she conducts research and teaches literacy courses to graduate students. She is a former elementary school teacher and has taught in both urban and rural settings. Since 1999 she has studied beginning reading materials and text difficulty. Dr. Mesmer has worked extensively with schools and teachers in funded projects. She was a Spencer Foundation/National Academy of Education postdoctoral fellow and a recipient of an Institute of Education Sciences/ American Educational Research Association grant.

# Preface

Any book that helps a child to form a habit of reading, to make reading one of his deep and continuing needs, is good for him.
—MAYA ANGELOU

As Maya Angelou reminds us, bringing kids and books together will have far-reaching, often life-changing consequences. Strong literacy teachers take very seriously their responsibility to establish lifelong habits of reading. They know that getting kids hooked on reading requires finding books that are both appealing and accessible. Since 1923, when the field saw the first readability formula, educators have wrangled with the process of judging the difficulty of children's reading materials (Klare, 1954). Across almost a century, processes for estimating book difficulty have changed and grown. What has remained stable is the interest that teachers have in using valid, reliable tools to bring appropriate books to children.

Several existing professional resource books address text difficulty. These books focus on readability formulas, qualitative leveling systems, or commercially available programs. However, most of the existing professional resource books describe and promote one particular system. These books rarely bring together information about many different tools for estimating text difficulty. Thus, these books do not help teachers and administrators become wise consumers of the *many different* systems now available. The goal for this book is to fill the gap for a usable resource that brings together information from many different sources. This book is for teachers, administrators, literacy coaches, reading specialists, library–media specialists, and graduate students. It has two major purposes: to provide basic information about the various tools, lists, programs, and systems that elementary teachers can use to estimate book difficulty, and to show educators how to use these systems effectively and appropriately.

Chapter 1 establishes the importance of matching readers with texts and describes the role of text analysis tools in making matches. Part I describes three different types of text analysis tools: classic readability formulas, second-generation readability formulas, and beginning reading materials. Chapter 2 gives an overview of traditional readability formulas. Because of their history and influence, traditional readability formulas are foundational to understanding the analysis of text difficulty. Chapter 3 describes recent electronic enhancements to traditional readability formulas, enhancements that continue the traditional formats to a second generation. These have fundamentally changed the nature of readability formulas. An example would be the Lexile system, which is theoretically based on readability. Chapter 4 discusses systems for beginning readers. These include qualitative leveling systems, decodability, and vocabulary control. Each of these approaches to text difficulty addresses distinct sources of support for the beginner, and each suits specific instructional purposes. Chapters 2 through 4 provide brief descriptions of the systems and include relevant charts, tables, and graphs. The goal of these chapters is to provide basic information.

Part II describes how teachers and schools successfully use text analysis tools. Chapter 5 discusses how three schools used text analysis tools to help teachers match readers with texts. This chapter describes why schools would want to establish a schoolwide system, and it includes a five-step process that schools can use for choosing text analysis tools. The chapter also examines how a literacy coach reorganized her school's bookroom and how a library–media specialist worked with teachers in her building to facilitate text–reader matching in the library. The chapter includes important questions that schools should ask themselves before making purchases. Chapter 6 describes how primary teachers have used text analysis tools in real classrooms. This chapter shows how to connect materials with the specific developmental needs of readers. Chapter 7 describes intermediate teachers' uses of text analysis tools. Through a series of vignettes, the chapter describes how teachers organize books for independent self-selected reading, communicate with parents, and choose trade materials for instruction.

The Appendix focuses on a set of very popular *applications* of text analysis tools: electronic book-matching programs like Accelerated Reader or Reading Counts. Technically, these programs are not text analysis tools, but they rely on text analysis tools, and teachers consistently ask me about these systems when I conduct workshops or give presentations.

During the past 9 years, I have spent a great deal of time working with schools and teachers in Florida, Virginia, and Oklahoma. Under the auspices of the Reading Excellence Act, the No Child Left Behind Act, and several Professional Development School partnerships, I have learned a great deal about text–reader matching. My funded research projects have taken me to rural and urban school sites and child care centers investigating the nature of instructional materials. In clinical supervision at Oklahoma State University's Randall and Carol White Reading and Math Center, I have discovered that finding the appropriate text for each reader is a significant problem faced by both experienced and inexperienced teachers. Across many contexts and in at least three different geographic regions, I have found that too many children are simply reading books that are not appropriate. Sadly, in many classrooms, all students are provided with the same reading materials, and there is no differentiation. I believe that these mismatches are occurring because text analysis is not receiving adequate attention in the professional literature. I study textual supports because I feel strongly that they are an important part of the literacy equation (Mesmer, 1999, 2001a, 2001b, 2004, 2005). My hope is that this book will improve reading for the children who depend on it most, and that the information provided here will support teachers whose professional work is dedicated to helping children to learn to read.

## ACKNOWLEDGMENTS

I wish to acknowledge the reviewers whose constructive criticism significantly improved the quality of this work. In addition, I thank Judy Richardson, Thomas Gunning, Sharon Walpole, and Barbara Walker, who provided feedback on various chapters. I also thank Chris Jennison, Publisher, Education, for his patience and support throughout this project, and thank as well Editorial Assistant Natalie Graham and Production Editor Anna Nelson, and all the professional staff at The Guilford Press. Finally, I thank my husband, Eric.

# Contents

# CHAPTER 1

# Using Text Analysis Tools to Match Readers to Texts

**Match:** to fit together, to harmonize with
—Webster's Ninth New
Collegiate Dictionary

In matching readers to texts, teachers are hoping to create not only a good fit between text and reader but also harmony—a pleasing arrangement. An appropriate match will make the difference between a child becoming a confident, skilled reader or a frustrated, declining reader. In fact, research indicates that when readers spend a great deal of time reading appropriate texts, they will become fluent, acquire more words, and exponentially increase their skills (Stanovich, 1985). Conversely, when they do not read a great deal or do not have manageable books, they will increasingly fall behind their peers (Stanovich, 1985). The more that children read, the better they get; the better they get, the more they are able to read.

So important is matching readers to texts that Allington (2005) has identified this instructional process as one of the missing pillars of effective reading instruction. Regrettably, he points out, this instructional non-negotiable has been overshadowed by other agendas. Allington writes, "All pupils need texts of an appropriate level of complexity in their hands all day long" (2005, p. 1). *Standards for Reading Professionals* (International Reading Association, 2004) emphasizes the importance of selecting materials for readers. Standard 4.1 stresses the importance of reading specialists and literacy coaches in "assisting the classroom teacher and paraprofessional in selecting materials that match the reading levels, interests, and cultural and linguistic background of students" (International Reading Association, 2004, p. 10). The text–reader match is particularly serious for struggling readers who often receive instruction in texts that are too difficult (Allington, 2001; Atkinson, Wilhite, Frey, & Williams, 2002; Biancarosa & Snow, 2004; O'Connor et al., 2002). Sometimes struggling readers appear to plod through (or pretend to read) class novels or basals, but they will not reap instructional benefits from reading materials that are too difficult. Children instructed at frustrational levels will experience increased exasperation, destroyed motivation, and depleted self-esteem. Children who have successful and interesting experiences with books are more likely to be motivated to read again (Guthrie et al., 2006; Ozgungor & Guthrie, 2004; Wigfield, Guthrie, Tonks, & Perencevich, 2004). Children who fail to read books fluently are more likely to avoid reading. Some will never freely pick up a book in their lives. Many will personalize their reading failures, believing that they are incompetent and dull.

Another reason why text–reader matching is so important is that many elementary learners have difficulty selecting materials for themselves (Donovan, Smolkin, & Lomax, 2000; Fresch, 1995). They are often unsure of how to judge the difficulty of books and may select books that are too hard or may cling to very easy texts. Beginning readers require guidance from the adults in their lives to help them find books. In essence, matching elementary readers with texts greatly affects the educational and social–emotional outcomes for them.

## ELEMENTS OF READER–TEXT MATCHING

To match a reader to text, teachers must connect information about readers with information about texts. Figure 1.1 illustrates both the text and reader factors that come together when teachers make text selections. First, a teacher must consider the reader and her abilities, motivation, and knowledge (Rand Reading Study Group, 2002). Readers will have differing reading levels, attention spans, and memory. Knowing the reading levels of elementary students is especially important because their reading abilities grow and change vastly across the elementary years. Teachers ascertain reading levels using assessments like informal reading inventories, basal assessments, standardized tests, running records, computer programs, and careful observation. Also in the elementary years, children have varying levels of attention and concentration. As readers grow and change, they can increasingly focus on more

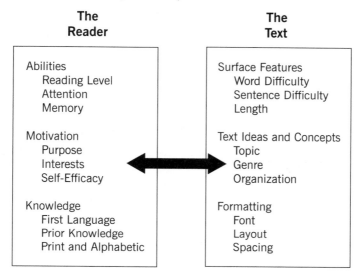

**FIGURE 1.1.** Text and reader factors in text–reader matching.

extended texts and persist in more challenging reading tasks. A reader's task persistence is a factor in matching him or her with an appropriate text. The reader's memory will also enter into identifying appropriate books. When readers develop a memory for larger stores of words, they can handle more difficult materials.

Although it has not received a great deal of attention, motivation is a critical reader factor (Cassidy & Cassidy, 2003; Guthrie et al., 2006). Readers' purposes will influence their motivations for reading. When readers focus on enjoyment, they read differently than if they are required to retain information from a text (Rosenblatt, 2004). When reading for enjoyment, readers are savoring the feelings, senses, or perceptions that the text offers. When reading to acquire text information, they are visualizing, note taking, and prioritizing information in text. Interests will also carry weight in text–reader matches. Often readers can handle texts that are a little more difficult if they have a keen interest in the topic. Materials that do not coincide with readers' interests will be more difficult. Last, readers' self-perceptions will shape their motivations. Readers who possess lower esteem will be less likely to persist in a task, even within their ability level, than readers with stronger self-images.

Readers' knowledge about language, the world, and print will impact how they interact with a text. Since 1979, the number of school-age children who speak a language other than English at home increased from 9% to 19% of the total school-age population (National Center for Education Statistics, 2005). English language learners require special considerations because English language texts might contain unfamiliar words or difficult academic vocabulary. These children may even require materials in their native languages. Another important reader factor is background or prior knowledge. Some children come to school with many diverse experiences, rich oral vocabularies, and familiarity with books. Others arrive with far less information about how books work, far fewer experiences, and less oral language (Hart & Risley, 1995). The prior knowledge that children have will significantly affect how they read and comprehend a text. Finally, a reader's stage of development will also enter into the match. Readers who are just learning about alphabetics will require fundamentally different materials than those who are more fluent. Developmental stages of readers will shape teachers' instructional goals and thereby influence text selections. When I am working with first graders, I usually try to find books that will match their levels of alphabetic knowledge and word recognition skills. However, when I am working with intermediate readers, I look for books that will enable fluency and comprehension.

For years, educators have used the term *readability* to describe all the text features that influence how a person reads and understands a book (Chall & Dale, 1995; Klare, 1963, 1988; Harris & Hodges, 1995; Harrison, 1980; Zakaluk & Samuels, 1988). Readability may include many different features; addressed here are surface features (wording), text ideas, and formatting. Because readers must recognize words to comprehend them, word difficulty is one of the first surface features that affects readability. We know that readers must be able to recognize about 95% of the words in a text in order to independently handle and comprehend the material (Clay, 1993; Gambrell, Wilson, & Gantt, 1981). With teacher or parent support, readers should be able to recognize 90–94% of the words. Teachers must be able to forecast whether most of the words in the book will be recognizable and understandable to readers. Researchers have predicted word difficulty by considering word length, meaning, frequency, or letter–sound complexity. As detailed later, the prediction of word difficulty has a long past.

A second surface feature in determining text difficulty is sentence complexity. Usually, longer sentences that include many relationships require readers to infer more information than shorter sentences. Book length can also affect difficulty. From first to fifth grade, elementary readers transition from very focused, slow word decoding to automatic, fluent reading. They progress from books of 10 pages that combine short sentences with supportive illustrations to books with chapters and hundreds of pages.

Anyone who has worked with a struggling intermediate-level reader knows that simply negotiating the surface features of a text is not sufficient for competent reading. The text ideas and concepts most certainly influence the difficulty of the material. At the very first level is the topic of the material. Texts focusing on complex and lesser known topics will be more difficult for students. The text's genre will also influence difficulty. Literary genres include narrative fiction, historical fiction, animal fantasy, high fantasy, science fiction, nonfiction, and poetry, among many others. Science fiction, for example, is a genre that presumes technical knowledge. If this presumed knowledge diverged from a reader's experiences, the material will be more difficult. Organization refers to the structure of a text. Simple texts possess straightforward, intuitive organizations with very few levels of organization. Complex texts can contain headings, subheadings, captions, and summaries. They may also contain chapters, indexes, glossaries, and tables of contents.

Text formatting also influences difficulty. Formatting includes fonts used, layout of the publication, and spacing. Font sizes and styles can make material difficult or easy. Larger fonts with very simple, manuscript-style letters are typically more accessible than tighter Roman-style fonts. Layout includes the coordination of print, graphics, and negative space (on the page). Simpler texts have straightforward designs at the book and page levels. At the book level, a simpler text may have a title page with body pages. At the page level, there is a balance between print and pictures and a highly consistent layout from page to page. Complex texts may include sidebars, different types of graphics, and less consistent layouts. A final formatting feature is spacing. Print-dense, tight spacing increases the difficulty of a material. Books with words that are spaced generously are easier.

Considering the many reader and text factors involved, text–reader matching is no simple task. In fact, the work of making a match does not conclude once a text has been selected. The arrow in Figure 1.1 represents the interaction between text and reader that occurs after text selection. Even though we can make informed matches, "the true test of readability ultimately resides within the interaction between reader and text" (Schirmer & Lockman, 2001, p. 39). This interaction will cause unexpected results, and we must carefully observe as children read and teach them to develop the same awareness.

My observations of Davis, a beginning reader, illustrate the unexpected results that can occur during text–reader matches. I have worked closely with Davis, and I have developed substantive knowledge about his literacy knowledge. Nonetheless, one day I chose a book that did not work for him. As I listened to Davis read, it became clear that the book was all wrong. I began tallying the words that he was missing. Proportionally, he needed help with about 20% of the words, meaning that he was reading the book with only 80% accuracy. When the reading was finished, I felt a lot like he did; deflated. I pointed out that he had worked really hard and that the book was a little tricky, and I put the book away. Later I flipped back through it. The book did not work for Davis for some very specific reasons: It had a number of long words, several complex proper nouns, two unusual contractions, and a topic that was unfamiliar. In this case, I knew the reader and thought I knew the text, but the "chemistry" between the two just wasn't there. Close, reflective teaching is an essential element of text–reader matching; without it, high-quality matches will not take place.

Sometimes I have witnessed text–reader matches that provide little challenge to the reader and subsequently limit the reader's learning opportunities. The result is a plateau in performance and often a loss of interest. In the reading clinic, we worked with Jeremy, a fourth grader who was reportedly struggling and unmotivated. To avoid frustrating Jeremy, his tutor initially chose books about one-half grade below his reading level. Unfortunately, the tutor used books at this level for too long, and Jeremy began to act bored, roll his eyes, and exert very little effort. In addition, he paid little attention to the books that he was reading and sometimes failed to answer very simple questions about them. We realized that the texts were actually independent-level materials and that we were not making the best use of the instructional time that we had.

In matching readers with texts, we want to strive to build the reader's skill in handling increasingly difficult texts. To do so, we must gradually select books that progressively increase in difficulty. Then we must support readers in accessing those texts. Vygotsky (1978) called this process *scaffolding*, and it refers to teaching within a zone of proximal development. This is the learning space between that which a learner can do completely independently and that which she cannot do even with assistance. By teaching in this zone, teachers enable students to attain higher levels of functioning. One often-forgotten element of this theory, however, is that the entire purpose of teaching "in the zone" is to continue to challenge learners so that they gradually are able to perform tasks that were previously beyond their range. In other words, teaching slightly difficult material with support should shift a student's ability. The same principle holds true with books, as illustrated in Figure 1.2. When a teacher selects a book for instruction, it should provide optimal challenge. The solid arrows and the space between them mark

## Zone of Proximal Development

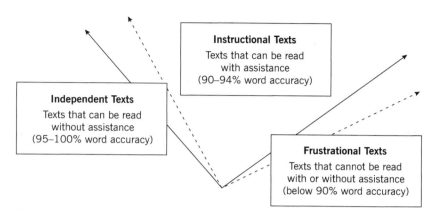

**FIGURE 1.2.** Text choices in the zone of proximal development.

the range of books that a child might be able to read initially with help. These are instructional-level materials. Materials in the area left of the arrow are independent materials that the reader can access with no help, and materials that fall in the zone to the right of the arrow are frustrational materials. The dashed arrows signify a shift in the zone of proximal development as a reader develops and is continually challenged. Gradually, books that were previously frustrational become accessible with assistance (instructional) and then accessible without assistance (independent). Books that are read without support during free reading or take-home reading should be in the independent range. Text analysis tools assist teachers in identifying texts that fall into the independent and instructional levels.

## TEXT ANALYSIS TOOLS

Although each element of the text–reader match is important, this book focuses primarily on the measurement of *text factors* or *readability*. The term *text analysis tool* is used throughout this book to refer to the many mechanisms that estimate the difficulty of books. Text levels can be expressed using many different metrics. The most typical are grade levels expressed in grades and tenths (e.g., 2.3) or Guided Reading Levels expressed in letters (e.g., A, B, and C). Increasingly, I am also seeing schools use Lexiles expressed in Lexile units (e.g., 120L or 500L). All of these tools help teachers begin the matching process, but they all have shortcomings. As a former third-grade teacher and current university faculty member, I have observed a love–hate relationship with text analysis tools. Although these tools are necessary and often helpful, they can be misinterpreted and misused. An experience that I had with an urban elementary school illustrates this point.

One summer I worked with teachers and a literacy coach to select reading materials. The funds for purchasing materials had to be spent quickly, so we sat down one afternoon with five catalogues in front of us and began what we thought would be a simple (and fun!) task. We wanted to select instructional materials that could supplement the basal reading series in grades K through 5. As we perused the catalogues, we became mired in numbers, letters, and other labels used to designate text difficulty.

One catalogue reported the difficulty of materials using standard grade levels. Books came in sets with a specific grade range (e.g., reading levels 1.0 to 1.5). Another company reported text difficulty using five different designations: (1) Reading Recovery numbers; (2) Guided Reading or Fountas–Pinnell letters; (3) Developmental Reading Assessment numbers; (4) color names used by the publisher (e.g., silver, gold, emerald); and (5) catalogue labels used by the publisher (e.g., "emergent," "early," "early fluent," and "fluent"). Still another company added to the mix their own leveling system using letters that did not correspond with the Guided Reading levels. As we talked to each other, we became confused by these many symbols. The simple and necessary task of determining text difficulty had been transformed into a veritable conundrum. By the end of the day, we were howling at the absurdities of all the different letters, numbers, and colors. Beneath our good humor, however, was a layer of genuine concern. Although we were able to piece together bits of information about these labels based on our collective knowledge, individually our grasp of each of these systems was tentative at best.

The experience left me with two thoughts. First, the diversity of labels amazed me. Clearly, some of the labels were idiosyncrasies of particular publishing houses, but still a range of legitimate and widely used systems existed. My second insight was that it could be easy to misinterpret the various difficulty labels, and the result could be expensive. The experience impressed upon me the importance of having a basic understanding of these labels. All text analysis tools exist for the purpose of estimating text difficulty. However, not all tools consistently address the same text elements. Some focus a bit more on content, whereas others focus on word difficulty. Different tools can coordinate with different purposes. Some systems make very fine distinctions between texts, distinctions more appropriate at the very beginning stages of reading. Other tools are more applicable to ranges above the first grade. The key to using these tools is unlocking how each appraises text difficulty and then matching the tool, and resulting text difficulty label, with the readers' needs.

After my experiences with these teachers, I discovered many other text analysis tools. Figure 1.3 highlights some of the major text analysis tools developed since the 1930s. The timeline shows tools in the three categories described in this book: traditional readability formulas, second-generation readability formulas, and the beginning reading scaffolds of vocabulary control, decodability, and qualitative leveling systems. The timeline reveals that text analysis tools have had a long history and continue to develop today.

In summary, putting the right books in the hands of children can make or break their literacy development. Despite this imperative, little attention has been given to matching readers with texts or understanding available tools. There are a number of text analysis tools and, unfortunately, a great deal of misunderstanding about what various labels mean. In addition, some states mandate exactly how text difficulty must be established, compromising professional autonomy. The purposes of this book are to inform the profession about the workings of the most popular text analysis tools and to show school personnel how to use these tools. Educators who are informed can make choices and select tools that best meet the needs of their students.

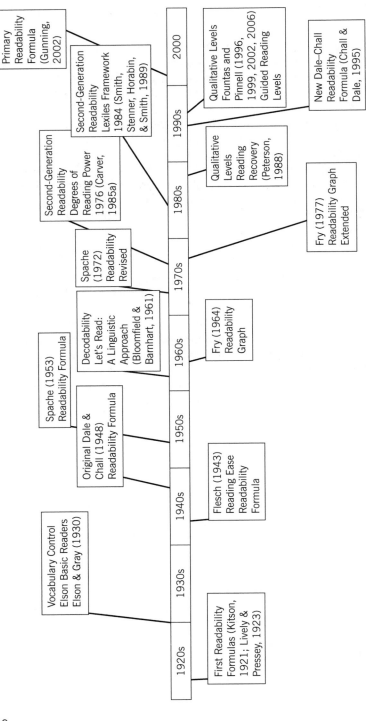

**FIGURE 1.3.** Highlights in the development of text analysis tools.

# PART I

# TEXT ANALYSIS TOOLS
*A Reference*

# CHAPTER 2

# Traditional
# Readability Formulas

There is no safety in numbers, or in anything else.
—JAMES THURBER

Traditional readability formulas have been with us since the 1920s (Klare, 1954). The results of these formulas, expressing text difficulty in grades and tenths (e.g., 2.3, 4.5, 6.1), can be found on the back covers of paperbacks, bundled within popular software packages, and reported on the World Wide Web. In fact, readability formulas are in education, industry, government, and mass communications. Perhaps because of their ubiquity, readability formulas and the numerical estimates they provide have often been misinterpreted, misused, and misunderstood. As James Thurber dryly reminds us, numbers, including the ones generated by readability formulas, are no safer than any other estimates of text difficulty.

Chapter 1 stressed the importance of understanding text analysis tools in matching readers and texts. This chapter begins with traditional readability formulas for three reasons. First, they are long-standing and have an extensive history (Harrison, 1980; Klare, 1963). Understanding traditional readability formulas is foundational to understanding text analysis tools as a whole. Many current approaches to readability are a reaction to or an improvement of traditional readability formulas. Designers of newer tools like Lexiles and Degrees of Reading Power have based their work on traditional readability formulas. In addition, formulas are also commonly used in informal reading inventories, standardized reading assessments, basal reading series, and other educational products. Thus, traditional readability formulas represent both the past and, in many cases, the present of text analysis.

In addition, an understanding of the traditional readability formulas is key because the grade-level estimates they provide can be deceiving. The numerically expressed grade levels seem so exact and appealing, but in reality, they are simply rough estimates expressed in mathematical terms. When educators understand how the grade-level estimates are derived, they can understand that these estimates represent only a part of what makes a text readable. Last, in my work with preservice teachers, teachers, and graduate students, I've seen that readability formulas can be easily misapplied. Sometimes people use formulas with an inadequate sample, apply the formulas to inappropriate materials, or select the wrong formula for the level of the text they are analyzing.

At one professional conference, a group of teachers approached me to discuss their analysis of a set of reading passages. As reflective professionals, they had decided to investigate the difficulty of a set of passages from a popular reading assessment. After using the assessment, they found a few of the passages to be either too high or too low a level for their students. They conducted a readability analysis on the passages and, to their surprise, the analysis indicated that the *all* of the passages were between one and two grade levels higher than labeled. These teachers were understandably concerned. When they told me about the web-based readability calculator that they had used, I realized that their results were inaccurate because they had not selected the appropriate formula from a drop-down menu. Their skewed results were a consequence of using a formula better suited for upper elementary grades. The formula that they used had a measurement range beginning at a grade higher than the grade they were teaching. No matter what material they analyzed, the formula would not give a result below a certain grade level. Their results were inflated because of the formula they were using. To use readability formulas and draw appropriate conclusions about their results, teachers need some basic information.

This chapter addresses the basics of readability formulas in two sections. Many authors and researchers have written about readability. This chapter only scratches the surface. The section first provides an overview of readability formulas, describing generally how they work, the text features used for prediction, and the research base. This is followed by a brief overview of five of the most common readability formulas and guidelines for using them.

# AN OVERVIEW OF READABILITY FORMULAS

As detailed by Harris and Hodges (1995) in *The Literacy Dictionary*, readability formulas are "any of a number of objective methods of estimating or predicting the difficulty level of reading materials by analyzing the samples from them with results usually expressed as a reading grade level" (p. 205).

Readability formulas are objective and are based on measurable features of writing (Venable, 2003). They focus on features of text that can be collected impartially, such as the number of words in a sentence or the number of syllables in a word. The formulas are designed to be objective rather than subjective to enhance reliability. If I asked two people to estimate the difficulty of a book entitled *Snow*, their estimates would depend on a number of different subjective factors. A teacher in Florida might find the vocabulary in the book—words like *drift, bank, flurry,* and *blizzard*—to be complex and to require a great deal of explanation. On the other hand, a teacher in Michigan might assume many of these words to be simple. This is an example of a subjective measurement, one influenced by individual judgment, experiences, and bias. Readability formulas overcome these issues but create others.

Readability formulas are mathematical equations that estimate how difficult a material will be for an intended audience. The purpose is to predict how hard the material will be without actually asking readers to read the materials themselves. The formulas allow you to take a text sample from a book, count certain text features of the sample, and then factor the feature information into a formula to obtain the estimated grade level. To illustrate, the Flesch–Kincaid formula (Kincaid, Fishburne, Rogers, & Chissom, 1975) is shown below:

$$(0.39 * \text{average words/sentence}) + (11.8 * \text{average syllables/word}) - 15.9$$

The following 53-word text sample from *Lilly's Purple Plastic Purse* (Henkes, 1996), taken from the middle of the book, illustrates how to use a readability formula. (For the purposes of this example, only 53 words are used, but at least 150 words would be used for an authentic application of any formula.)

> Whenever the students had free time, they were permitted to go to the Light bulb Lab in the back of the classroom. They expressed their ideas creatively through drawing and writing. Lilly went often. She had a lot of ideas. She drew pictures of Mr. Slinger. And she wrote stories about him, too. (Henkes, 1996, p. 6)

To use this formula, one simply calculates the average number of words per sentence in the text sample—8.3 in this sample—and multiplies by constant 0.39. This result is added to the average number of syllables per word in the text sample. There are 73 syllables in this text sample and 53 words, yielding an average of 1.37 syllables per word. This result (1.37) is multiplied by the constant 11.8. From the addition of the words–sentence variable and the syllables per word variable, one subtracts 15.9 to obtain a grade-level estimate for the materials. In this case, the estimate is 03.49, or third grade.

- Step 1.   [(0.39 * 8.3) + (11.8 * 1.37)] – 15.9 = *grade level estimate*
- Step 2.   (3.237 + 16.16) – 15.9 = grade level estimate
- Step 3.   19.397 – 15.9 = 3.497 grade level estimate

(Interestingly, this estimate illustrates the limitations that readability formulas have with primary materials, discussed in Chapters 4 and 6.) The purpose of this illustration is to demonstrate how formulas work. Keep in mind that this example is purely illustrative and that a much more complete text sample would yield a better estimate of difficulty. Other readability formulas work the same way.

Readability formulas provide *estimates* of difficulty. The reading level obtained from a formula is a ballpark figure for understanding the difficulty level of a book. Noted readability researcher Klare (1988), called the estimates *probability statements*. A book with a reading level of 2.3 will probably be most appropriate for a reader in the first half of second grade. However, depending on the child, the circumstance, and the measurement error, the book may be appropriate at different times. Importantly, readability formulas only measure a small portion of that which makes a book readable. Just as tests of intelligence assume that the actual construct of intelligence is larger, more comprehensive, and more dynamic than tests can measure, so also is readability more comprehensive than that which readability formulas can measure (Chall & Dale, 1995).

The history of readability formulas is both deep and broad. As described in the research section of this chapter, formulas have been researched deeply, but they have also been applied broadly. Researchers, testing companies, writers, government agencies, industries, librarians, and teachers have relied on formulas for years. In documents such as *Guide to Air Force Writing* (Department of the Air Force, 1953), formula developers shaped military training documents or assessed the reading levels necessary for particular military specialties (Caylor, Sticht, Fox, & Ford, 1973). Government has used formulas in assessing the difficulty of forms and documents. Journalists have deployed readability formulas to reach the masses through newspapers (Flesch, 1943; Gunning, 1968). Test developers require formulas to equate the difficulty of passages in assessments (Oakland & Lane, 2004). Librarians use readability formulas to help readers find suitable materials (Fry, 2002; Schade, 2004). Industries use readability formulas to analyze training materials and consumer labels. Hospitals and public health entities use formulas to analyze insurance policies, patient directives, and drug labels (Walfish & Watkins, 2005). Teachers, of course, use readability formulas to analyze children's literature, textbooks, and content area materials. Readability formulas exist for French, Dutch, Spanish, Hebrew, German, Hindi, Russian, and Chinese languages (Klare, 1988).

Understanding the broad applications of formulas is not immediately applicable in the classroom, but teachers and university students usually find formulas more credible when they understand their extensive use in other arenas. Furthermore, this information helps in appreciating the converging research base for readability formulas.

## Text Features

When readability formulas were first developed, researchers measured as many as 100 different elements of writing (for a full review, see Chall & Dale, 1995; Harrison, 1980; Klare, 1963; Zakaluk & Samuels, 1988). They tried features such as number of prepositional phrases, length of sentences, number of personal pronouns, number of dependent clauses or phrases, number of sentences, and number of independent clauses, to name a few. After decades of readability research, developers settled on two features that worked best in predicting text difficulty: word-level difficulty, or semantic complexity, and sentence difficulty, or syntactic difficulty. Repeatedly, when researchers attempted to enhance formulas with text features beyond these two, they found little benefit in prediction to the cost of additional effort.

With only this information about readability formulas, some limitations are immediately evident. Although quantifiable text features promote reliability in formula results, they will not capture ideas in a text, topics, or writing style. Words and sentences only compose surface features of the text, and they do not stand alone. Text is organized into paragraphs and then into sections or chapters. Sentences build upon one another.

### Semantic Difficulty

Formula developers used one of two different indices to estimate word difficulty: word lists or word length. Formulas that used word lists are sometimes called vocabulary-based formulas. The Dale–Chall, Spache, and Primary Readability formulas, discussed later, are all vocabulary based. These formulas compare words in a passage to the formula's list of easy words. Then the number of hard words in the passage (those not on the list) is factored into the formula. The most valid way of identifying easy words for formulas is testing students' knowledge of the words. For instance, Chall and Dale (1995), for their formula, compiled a list of words known to 80% of fourth graders. The fact that the list is based on the performance of students adds to the validity of the formula. Biemiller (2006) devised lists of words known to readers at grades 2, 4, 6, 8, 10, and 12, although these lists have not been used in formulas.

Because validation with students is costly, developers have relied on print frequency to compile word lists. They treated high-frequency words as easy and low-frequency words as hard. Developers usually set a cutoff to separate high-frequency and low-frequency words and then compile word lists. Words meeting a certain standard for frequency make it onto the lists and less frequent words do not. In one that I analyzed, the word *delicious* occurred 117 times in 2.5 million words. In contrast, the word *later* occurred 992 times (Mesmer, 2007). If I were using these word frequencies to create a list of easy words, I might set a cutoff of 1,000 occurrences and include on my formula's list only words that occurred at least 1,000 times.

Of course, the word list is at the heart of any vocabulary-based formula. The formula's results will only be as good as the list itself. Word lists do have limitations, however. Lists that are dated (and some are), highly exclusive, or highly inclusive will influence the results. A lengthy, inclusive list may underestimate text difficulty because the reader is expected to know many words. A short, restrictive list may overestimate text difficulty because the reader is not presumed to know as many words. Sometimes words excluded from lists are rare but not difficult (Adams, 2001). In Adams's analysis of a sample of 5 million words in elementary texts, the words, *magnanimous, send, smock, loquacious, ingots,* and *gag* all had the same frequency. Each of these words appeared only twice. Despite this fact, *magnanimous,* a four-syllable word meaning generous, is clearly both difficult and rare while *smock* is more rare than difficult. The other problem with vocabulary-based formulas is that any word not on the list will increase the difficulty. In most vocabulary-based formulas, names and places are only counted once to avoid this inflation. However, if a hard word is repeated, then the level will also be inflated even though the repetition may actually render the word easier to the reader. The General Considerations section addresses over- and underestimation of difficulty with vocabulary-based formulas.

Developers began using word length in an effort to make formulas more convenient. After extensive research, Zipf (1935) found that word length and word frequency are related. Shorter words are more frequent than longer words. For this reason, some formulas include syllable counts or letter counts as a different proxy for word difficulty. The Fry and the Flesch–Kincaid formulas, described later, both use word length in syllables. Vocabulary-based formulas are a bit more predictive of readability than those that use word length because word length is actually a proxy for frequency, which is itself a proxy for difficulty (Chall & Dale, 1995; Klare, 1963).

## Sentence Difficulty

To estimate sentence difficulty, formula developers take into account the number of words in a sentence because longer sentences are usually more complex. Take, for instance, the sentence "The dog ran" compared with the sentence "In the blink of an eye, the small, brown dog ran across the snow-covered pasture toward the spry fox." The first sentence is shorter and contains far fewer relationships between words. It is far less complex than the second. To find the subject–predicate nucleus of the second sentence, "the dog ran," the reader must sort through adjectives and phrases. The second sentence contains four prepositional phrases.

All of the formulas reviewed in the latter part of this chapter approximate semantic difficulty using sentence length. Developers normally use final punctuation as a guide for determining where sentences end. Sentence length is a less robust predictor of syntactic difficulty than word-level semantic indicators. In previous work, when word-level and sentence-level variables were entered singly into prediction equations, the word-level indicators were more powerful, and this held true in languages other than English (Cohen & Steinberg, 1983; Klare, 1963, 1988). The sentence-level variables improve prediction enough to be useful but are still less helpful than the semantic indicators. Measuring sentence length to approximate syntax also assumes that the author has written syntactically valid sentences because technically a word count could be obtained on any collection of words. For example, the word count in the syntactically correct sentence "I went to the store" is the same as the word count in the sentence, "To went I store the."

## Processes for Using Text Features to Predict Text Difficulty

In order to design a usable formula, developers must relate the information about text features to some established criterion of text difficulty.

For example, on average *The Snowy Day* (Keats, 1962) contains 10.2 words per sentence and 4.1 letters per word. As a second-grade teacher, I would think, "Well, that's nice, but what does that tell me about the difficulty of *The Snowy Day*? How many words per sentence do materials at the second-grade level typically have?"

The formula developer starts with known information about text difficulty, collects information about text features, and then distills this information into a formula that explains the relationship between text features and difficulty. Most developers also transform their formula results into a grade-level metric. The resulting readability formula becomes a tool for estimating the difficulty of new books. Figure 2.1 illustrates the design process. Developers begin by collecting information about the text features in a book. Depending on the semantic indicators, they will measure the mean word length or compare words with those on a list. The developers will also measure sentence length. Developers collect samples of text from many books. These samples may include a page of the book, a specified number of words, or even the entire book.

The second step is to use the text features to predict the established difficulty for each book. The criteria to determine difficulty could include (1) the reading levels delivered by other readability formulas; (2) the difficulty ratings of teachers; (3) the grade level assigned by a basal reader; (4) the percentage of errors readers produce while reading the

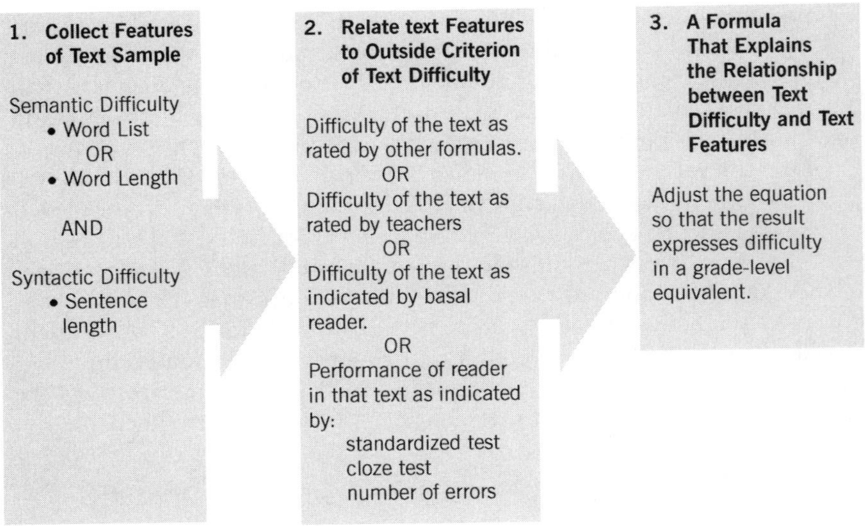

**FIGURE 2.1.** Process of designing a readability formula.

text; (5) the performance of readers on standardized tests; and (6) the performance of readers in completing cloze tests (see box in Chapter 3 for a description of cloze). The best equation for predicting difficulty becomes the readability formula, which is then adjusted to transform the equation's result into grade-level equivalents.

When teachers understand readability formulas, they are informed and can ask important questions. For example, the results of a formula will depend on how representative the text sample is. When only 300 words are taken from a large chapter book, the sample may not be completely typical. Larger samples more closely represent the actual book. Another important issue with the formulas is the criterion used for calibrating the formula. If a developer simply uses the results of another formula to design his own, then he is assuming the infallibility of the criterion formula. The process is circular, and the newly developed formula may not be much better than the old formula. Formulas built on the performance of students seem to be more valid because they do not piggyback on the results of previous formulas.

## RESEARCH ON READABILITY

This overview addresses two major eras in readability research: development and critical research. However, as readability expert Klare (1974) writes, "The history of readability is exhaustive" (p. 15). This chapter purposefully avoids the tedious details. The overview of research might be likened to a walking tour with a guide walking past historical structures and describing their contents. This review by no means enters the houses to examine the details and contents of each.

### Development and Refinement of Readability Formulas

The first readability formulas have been attributed to Lively and Pressey (1923) and to Kitson (1921), who developed formulas in the 1920s (Klare, 1963). During this time, teachers were dealing with a population of junior and senior high students who were the first in their families to complete secondary school (Chall, 1988). To meet the needs of these students with diverse educational abilities, teachers needed ways to assess the difficulty of science and social studies texts. Between 1923 and 1938 researchers furiously developed formulas (Klare, 1963). During this time, they tested the predictive power of many different text features. By 1938, research had shifted from formula development to simplification and increasing ease of use. The period between 1938 and 1953 produced many of the formulas discussed later in this chapter, such as the

Flesch–Kincaid, original Dale–Chall, and Spache. After 1953, researchers focused on specializing formulas for specific purposes or languages. Developers created formulas for use with standardized tests, test directions, primary-grade materials, and adults.

Also in the early 1950s, researchers examined various criteria. Most formula developers had used the McCall–Crabbs passages published originally in 1925 and then revised in 1950, 1961, and 1979. According to Klare (1988), these lessons "have been convenient statistically because there are a large number of reading passages, covering a wide range of difficulty, resting upon extensive testing, and providing detailed grade scores" (p. 66). In 1953, Taylor introduced cloze procedures, which were then revised by Bormuth in 1969. Eventually, grade levels became the most practical way to assign texts to readers. In the periods after initial development and refinement, researchers began discovering the shortcomings of readability formulas and embarked on more critical research.

## Critical Research of Readability Formulas

As early as the 1960s, researchers raised concerns about readability formulas. Even though they delivered exact numerical estimates, the formulas were not so precise. According to Gunning (2003), most readability estimates were within one grade level about 85% of the time and sometimes varied up to two grade levels. In another study by Gunning (2000), book levels had to be adjusted almost one third of the time. In other words, one formula might indicate that a book is at a difficulty of 2.3, whereas another might indicate its difficulty to be about 3.3. Thus, the grade-level estimates more likely are ranges that extend one-half to one whole-grade level above and below the provided number. Most readability researchers suggest that teachers use formulas as a starting point for making text–reader matches but also use qualitative measures as well (Chall, Bissex, Conrad, & Harris-Staples, 1996; Chall & Dale, 1995; Weaver, 2000). The General Considerations section suggests additional factors and checklists to take into account when using readability formulas.

Sometimes readability formulas will properly sequence materials but not accurately estimate the difficulty of a text (Harris & Jacobson, 1978). This principle is called *goodness of fit* (Gunning, 2003). A formula may indicate that Book A is more difficult than Book B, but it might estimate the difficulty of Book B as grade 3, when in reality it is at a fifth-grade level. A second formula may indicate that Book A is more difficult than Book B but more accurately estimates the absolute difficulty of the book. For example, *Frog and Toad Together* is easier than

*Superfudge* (Blume, 1980), but it is not at a third-grade level. The Spache and Primary Readability formulas have better fits at the lower levels, whereas others, like the Dale–Chall, work better at higher levels. Readability formulas should not simply sequence materials but also estimate the degree to which a text might work for a reader at a particular level.

One of the great concerns about readability formulas is that textbook publishers have misused them to adapt materials. Researchers have found that when writers adapt existing materials, the changes made to the texts can actually make the books or passages less readable (Davison & Green, 1988; Davison & Kantor, 1982; Fry, 1989; Irwin, 1980; Pearson, 1974). Davison and Kantor (1982) analyzed original and adapted passages extracted from the SRA Reading Laboratory for middle-level readers. They found that adapters had removed difficult vocabulary or shortened sentences in order to produce lower readability estimates. For example, Pearson (1974) found that shortening sentences did not always increase clarity but instead robbed the prose of important connectives (see Table 2.1, "clause connection," for example). Table 2.1 details five different types of adaptations identified in the Davison and Kantor study, provides original illustrations of each adaptation type, and describes why these changes can make materials more difficult. Table 2.1 helps teachers to spot an adapted text. After seeing this chart, one fifth-grade social studies teacher told me, " I knew that our social studies text was weird. I would find myself trying to explain the text over and over after each unit. When I saw this chart, I immediately realized why the text was hard for the kids." What studies tell us is that rewriting materials to conform to readability formulas can actually make them harder. Readability expert Fry (1977) agrees: "You can cheat or artificially doctor writing to get a lower readability formula score, but you might not have changed the true readability much and you may have made it worse" (p. 77).

Additionally, science education researchers have examined the use of readability formulas with textbooks. They found that science textbooks, when analyzed using readability formulas, turn out to be quite difficult (Shymansky & Yore, 1979; Yore, Bisanz, & Hand, 2003). However, researchers also discovered that readability formulas can artificially inflate the difficulty of science textbooks because of the many technical terms. For example, a science text might have the word *photosynthesis,* a word not found on the Dale–Chall. Although this word is difficult, if the word is repeated, illustrated, and explained, it becomes less difficult. Unfortunately, each repetition of the unfamiliar word actually increases the readability estimate (Cohen & Sternberg, 1983). Science textbooks, and probably other content area materials as well,

**TABLE 2.1. Formula-Conforming Adaptations That Can Increase Difficulty**

| Type of alteration | Description | Example | Explanation |
|---|---|---|---|
| Clause connection | The adapter reduces the length of sentences and thus removes relationships within a sentence. | *Original:* Although she was cold she kept walking because she wanted to see her grandma.<br><br>*Adapted:* She kept walking. She was cold. She wanted to see her grandma. | The first sentence indicates that the reason the character kept walking despite the cold was *because* she wanted to see her grandma. With *because* removed, the character's motivation for walking in the cold is not explicit. |
| Topic and focus | The adapter shifts the focus of the passage by removing topic sentences or by reordering sentences. | *Original:* Butterflies go through four life stages to become the beautiful creatures that we admire. They begin their lives as tiny eggs . . . .<br><br>*Adapted:* Butterflies begin their lives as tiny eggs . . . | The topic sentence in the original version signals the reader that the paragraph will be about four life stages. When this sentence is removed, readers do not have that organizing structure with which to begin their reading. |
| Inference | The adapter removes information that may lead the reader to an incorrect inference. | *Original:* Today's aircraft carrier is amazingly large, like a small town of 5,000. While this many people may make a *small* town, it is a large number of bodies to carry over the open ocean.<br><br>*Adapted:* Today's aircraft carrier is like a small city of 5,000. | The removal of the phrase *amazingly large* in the second sentence and the retention of the word *small* could inaccurately lead the reader to infer that aircraft carriers were small, like small cities. A student who did not have a relative understanding that 5,000 people is actually a lot of people to have on a vessel might incorrectly infer that the aircraft carriers are relatively small. |

24

| Point of view | The adapter removes text that attributes information to particular sources or that suggests the author's stance on a topic. | *Original:* Allegedly, the man intended to steal money by improperly logging donations into the agency's records. *Adapted:* The man tried to steal money by not logging donations into the agency's records. | The word *allegedly* in the first sentence, suggests that the author does not fully believe that the man was trying to steal money. By using this word, the author suggests that the allegations have not been proven. When this word is removed, the author's stance is removed and the tone of the sentence suggests incontrovertible guilt. |
| Vocabulary | The adapter removes or rewords vocabulary that may not be commonly found on lists. | *Original:* In the South, wet tobacco was placed on the skin as an antidote for the venom of an insect sting. *Adapted:* In the South, wet tobacco was placed on the skin as a way to heal the burn of an insect sting. | The words *antidote* and *venom* were removed and replaced with a descriptive phrase. A better way to handle unusual words, without depriving the reader of the opportunity to learn them, is to use a descriptive appositive: "an antidote, or cure for the poison of insect stings." |

*Note.* The types of alterations are based on Davison and Kantor (1982).

should be examined for features that would simplify material but not be reflected in the results of a readability formula.

Because researchers have been examining readability formulas for almost 100 years, the research is comprehensive and reflects both the positive and negative aspects of formulas. Essentially, research firmly supports that sentence length and word difficulty provide viable mechanisms for estimating difficulty, but they are imperfect.

## COMMON READABILITY FORMULAS

Because there are so many readability formulas, this chapter describes only five of the most common: the New Dale–Chall Readability formula (Chall & Dale, 1995); the Fry readability graph (1969); the Flesch–Kincaid Grade Level and Flesch Reading Ease; the Spache (1972); and the Primary Readability formula (Gunning, 2002). A brief overview is provided for each formula, including the basic background, year of creation, subsequent revisions, word and sentence difficulty metrics, and advantages and disadvantages. Table 2.2 (on pp. 32–33) summarizes the formulas discussed.

### New Dale–Chall Readability Formula

The New Dale–Chall Readability formula is a revision of the 1948 formula. The most recent 1995 formula is the result of more than 50 years of study and research (Chall, 1956, 1958/1974, 1984, 1988; Dale & Chall, 1948; Chall & Dale, 1995). Dale and Chall applied the highest standards to testing and validating this formula, rendering it one of the most highly regarded (Gunning, 2003; Klare, 1988). The Dale–Chall delivers whole-grade estimates of reading levels from grades 1 to 4. Beginning at grade 5, the formula uses ranges (e.g., grades 5–6, grades 7–8). Word difficulty is estimated using the Dale–Chall list of 3,000 words known by 80% of fourth graders (revised in 1984). The words not on the Dale–Chall list are technical, specialized, or abstract words that tend to be learned in the fourth grade and upward. Sentence difficulty is calculated by counting the number of words in a sentence.

The advantages of the Dale–Chall are that it was thoroughly researched, carefully developed, and recently revised. Harrison (1980) found that the Dale–Chall did a good job of predicting text difficulty of materials at a grade level of 5 and higher. Designations varied by only one half of a grade level in his analysis. The disadvantage is that the Dale–Chall is not useful for materials at the first- and second-grade levels. Specifics can be found in *Readability Revisited: The New Dale–*

*Chall Readability Formula* (Chall & Dale, 1995). The OKAPI! website provides a readability calculator using the Dale–Chall formula (*www. interventioncentral.org*). Click on the right-hand side of the page on the label "Reading Probe Generator." Enter a 170-word text sample and select the Dale–Chall from the dropdown menu.

## Fry Readability Graph

In 1968, Fry published a succinct graph and directions for use to estimate the readability of materials. Fry created the graph while teaching reading in Uganda. He subsequently published the work in British journals. Since then, Fry extended the grade range of the graph, validated it for elementary materials, created a formula for shorter passages, and republished it many times (Fry, 1977, 2002). The Fry graph is very popular. Figure 2.2 shows the unique graph, which delivers whole-grade estimates of reading level. Word difficulty is estimated by the number of syllables in words, and sentence difficulty by the number of words in a sentence.

The Fry graph has several advantages. First, it is one of the few readability tools that is not copyrighted, and so it has been republished numerous times and is widely available. It is also quite simple, can be applied to a wide range of materials, and has a strong history. The beauty of the Fry graph is its parsimony. The one-page graph does not include tedious counting rules and directions. The disadvantages include its limited use for developing readers in grade 1 (Fry, 1977). The graph also contains "gray areas." If the intersection of the row and column falls in this space, then no grade-level score can be found, and the grade-level scores are invalid for the text being evaluated.

To estimate the readability of materials using the Fry graph, a user selects three 100-word samples from a book, counts the number of sentences in each sample, counts the number of syllables in each sample, averages the calculations from the three samples, and then compares these data with the graph. The user identifies the average number of sentences per 100 words on the left axis and the average number of syllables per 100 words on the top axis, and finds the point at which the row and column intersect to obtain the readability level.

## Flesch Formulas

The Flesch–Kincaid Grade Level and Flesch Reading Ease are variations of the Flesch Readability formula first published in 1943 (Flesch, 1943; Kincaid, Fishburne, Rogers, & Chissom, 1975). Both the Flesch Reading Ease and the Flesch–Kincaid Grade Level come with the popular

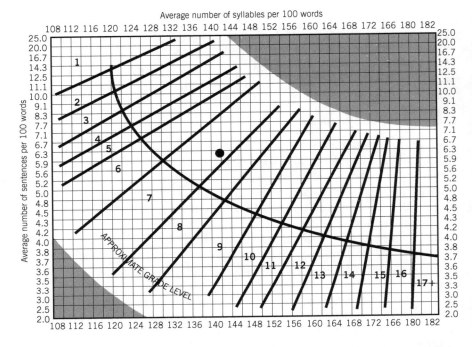

Average number of syllables per 100 words

Directions:  Randomly select 3 one hundred word passages from a book or an article. Plot average number of syllables and average number of sentences per 100 words on graph to determine the grade level of the material. Choose more passages per book if great variability is observed and conclude that the book has uneven readability. Few books will fall in gray area but when they do grade level scores are invalid.

Count proper nouns, numerals, and initialization as words. Count a syllable for each symbol. For example, "1945" is 1 word and 4 syllables and "IRA" is 1 word and 3 syllables.

| Example: | Syllables | Sentences |
|---|---|---|
| First hundred words | 124 | 6.6 |
| Second hundred words | 141 | 5.5 |
| Third hundred words | 158 | 6.8 |
| Average | 141 | 6.3 |

Readability seventh grade (see dot plotted on graph)

**FIGURE 2.2.**  Fry readability graph. From Fry (1969). In the public domain.

Microsoft Word software package. Flesch originally designed this formula for use in grade 3 and higher. Although the Grade Level formula will deliver results with a 0 grade level, it is still best used with upper elementary and secondary materials. The Reading Ease formula applies to adult materials no lower than fourth grade. Both formulas use average sentence length and average word length. The Reading Ease score is based on 100 points. Documents with scores closest to 100 are easiest. A difficult material with a score of 0 has more than 35 words per sentence, with most words containing at least two syllables. Writers striving for clarity and accessibility with an adult audience should set a Reading Ease score goal of about 65. The Flesch Reading Ease formula is

$$206.835 - (1.015* \text{ average words/sentence}) - (84.6* \text{ average syllables/word})$$

The Flesch–Kincaid Grade Level delivers grade levels from 0 to 17 on upper elementary materials. Although Flesch provides directions for manually applying both formulas, most readers will have access to Microsoft Word and can use the program to obtain estimates. Figure 2.3 describes how to access the readability statistics in Microsoft Word.

Both the Flesch–Kincaid Grade Level and the Flesch Reading Ease have advantages. First, they are very convenient. Because Microsoft Word is so widely used, these readability formulas are available to many people. With digital scanners that can copy text into a file, users can avoid typing text into a Microsoft Word file and simply obtain the read-

---

1. Type in three 100-word samples from the beginning, middle, and end of a document or book.
2. Configure Microsoft Word to calculate readability statistics.
   - Go to the Tools menu.
   - Click Options.
   - Click the Spelling and Grammar tab.
   - In the bottom left-hand corner, select the box that says "Show readability statistics."
3. Conduct a spell check. At the end of the spell check, a box entitled "Readability Statistics" will report Counts (words, characters, paragraphs, and sentences), Words, and Readability (percentage of passive sentences, Flesch Reading Ease, and Flesch–Kincaid Grade Level). The Flesch–Kincaid Grade Level will identify the readability level.

---

**FIGURE 2.3.** Directions for accessing the Flesch–Kincaid Grade Level and Flesch Reading Ease in Microsoft Word.

ability estimate. Because of the ease of application, users may be tempted to use the Flesch formulas heavily without considering their limitations. This, however, would be a mistake. The Flesch–Kincaid Grade Level is most useful with upper elementary materials, and even then it underestimates difficulty (Gunning, 2003).

## Spache Formula

In 1953, noting a gap in readability research, Spache designed a formula for grades 1 to 4. He later revised the formula in 1972. Like many others, Spache theorized that word difficulty represented the greatest challenge for beginning readers and therefore estimated word difficulty by the percentage of hard words, those not found on a list of 1,041 words. He estimated syntactic difficulty using the average number of words per sentence. Spache used basal reading materials as a criterion and reported a standard error of measurement of 3.3. A material with a grade level of 2.0 could have a true grade level as low as 1.7 or as high as 2.3. This tight range is especially advantageous for beginning readers, who can at least be equipped to cope with underestimations of difficulty. Like the Dale–Chall, the directions for applying the Spache manually require the user to compare the words encountered to word lists, tally the number of words not on the list, and obtain an average sentence length. Users then access a chart with average sentence length and number of hard words to obtain a difficulty level. The OKAPI! readability website can deliver Spache estimates (*www.interventioncentral.org*). The advantage of the Spache is that it works well with materials in grades 1 and 2. The Spache formula has two disadvantages. It underestimates difficulty at the third-grade level and above, and the word list has not been updated since 1974.

## Primary Readability Formula

Gunning (2002) devised the Primary Readability formula to accompany the Dale–Chall. The Primary Readability formula serves as an updated vocabulary-based formula and works with materials in grades 1 through 3. Gunning's vocabulary-based formula relies on average sentence length and a word list. The words not on the primary words list are considered hard words. This list comprises 810 words occurring with the highest frequency in first-grade materials based on *The Educator's Word Frequency Guide* (Zeno, Ivens, Millard, & Duwuri, 1995). The formula is:

$$(\text{Number of hard words} * 0.1519890) + (\text{Average sentence length} * 0.046509) + 0.980937$$

Complete directions can be found in *Assessing and Correcting Reading and Writing Difficulties* (Gunning, 2002). The Primary Readability formula also has a subjective factors element (Figure 2.4).

The advantage of the Primary Readability formula is that it is updated for use at grades 1 and 2. This vocabulary-based formula uses the most recent word list available. However, the formula is not widely available. A title listing of the readability of books using this formula is available in *Best Books for Building Literacy for Elementary School Children* (Gunning, 2000).

## Readability Resources

Table 2.2 summarizes important information about these five formulas. See box on p. 34 for information about three convenient resources for obtaining readability: (1) title listings; (2) computer software; and (3)

---

*Relationship of illustrations to text (check one)*

_____ Depict all of text
_____ Depict most of text
_____ Depict much of text
_____ Depict some of text
_____ Are simply supportive

*Difficulty of vocabulary and concepts*

_____ Familiar vocabulary and concepts
_____ One or two unfamiliar words or concepts
_____ Several unfamiliar words or concepts

*Decodability*

_____ Words not on list would be easy for students to decode
_____ Words not on list would be difficult for students to decode

*Structural aids to understanding*

_____ Little or no repetition
_____ Repetition of a phrase or sentence
_____ Repetition of a phrase or paragraph
_____ Use of rhyme

| | | | | | |
|---|---|---|---|---|---|
| Estimated interest level | \_\_\_\_ Low | \_\_\_\_ Medium | \_\_\_\_ High |
| Familiarity of topic or story line | \_\_\_\_ Low | \_\_\_\_ Medium | \_\_\_\_ High |
| Estimated difficulty level | | | |

**FIGURE 2.4.** The Primary Readability Formula: Subjective factors. From Gunning (2002). Copyright 2002 by Allyn & Bacon. Reprinted by permission.

**TABLE 2.2. An Overview of Common Readability Formulas**

| | New Dale–Chall | Fry graph | Flesch–Kincaid Grade Level | Spache | Primary Readability |
|---|---|---|---|---|---|
| First published | 1948 | 1964 | 1943 | 1953 | 2002 |
| Last updated | 1995 | 1977 | 1971 | 1974 | 2002 |
| Syntactic complexity—sentence | Average number of words per sentence | Average number of words per sentence | Average number of words per sentence | Average number of words per sentence | Average number of sentences per 100-word sample |
| Semantic complexity—words | Number of words not found on the New Dale–Chall List[a] | Number of syllables | Number of syllables | Number of words not on a list of 1,041 words from the Harris–Jacobson Basic Elementary Vocabulary | Number of words not on the Primary Word List: 810 frequently occurring first-grade words taken from *The Educator's Word List* |
| Validation methods | • Comparisons to other formulas Bormuth's passages (1971) • Gates–MacGinitie, NAEP passages | • Comprehension tests (unspecified) • Oral reading scores • Comparisons to other formulas • Comparisons to samples of basal readers[c] | • Comparisons to other formulas • Gates–MacGinitie Reading Test | • Comparisons to samples of basal readers[b] • Comparisons to other formulas | • Compared to the Fry and Spache using DRA passages (Beaver, 1997) |

32

| | | | | | |
|---|---|---|---|---|---|
| Increments used and grade range | Whole grades 1–4 Two-grade ranges for 5–16 (e.g., 5–6, 7–8) | Whole grades 1–17 | Grade Level: grades and tenths 0–12 (e.g., 1.2, 2.3) Reading Ease: 0–100 (0-hardest) | Whole grades and tenths 0.8 to 3.9 | Whole grades |
| Advantages | Recently revised Well validated Best estimates at grade 3+ | Not copyrighted Easy to use | Bundled with Microsoft Word | Best estimates at grades 1 and 2 | Best estimates at grades 1 and 2 Based on the latest word list (1995) |
| Disadvantages | Weaker estimates at grades 1–2 | Gray area on graph does not deliver estimates of readability | May underestimate Not good for grades 1 and 2 | Not recently revised Underestimates at grade 3+ | Best used with beginning reading materials |

*Note.* DRA, Developmental Reading Assessment; NAEP, National Assessment of Educational Progress.
[a]This list contains the 3,000 words known by 80% of students in grade 4.
[b]224 100-word samples from 152 primary basal readers.
[c]Work by Anne Fox applied the formula to all basal reading materials published in 1978.

## RESOURCES FOR READABILITY

- **Follett Publishing Company. (2000).** *The elementary school library collection.* **River Grove, IL: Author.**
  This annotated title listing includes "top picks" for a library collection. The listing uses the Spache readability formula for grades 1 and 2 and the Fry for materials at grade 3 and higher.

- **Gunning, T. G. (2000).** *The best books for beginning readers.* **Boston: Allyn & Bacon.**
  This book lists hundreds of titles for use with children in grades 1 through 3. The first chapters describe a subjective tool for indexing the books. The list is annotated and ordered by grade level. It includes a range of genres.

- **Readability Calculator Software by Micro Power and Light (*www.micropowerandlight.com*).**
  This software calculates the readability of a material with nine different formulas. It will accept a text sample of any size including scanned text and provides a helpful users' manual.

- **Readability Studio by Oleander Solutions (*www.oleandersolutions.com*).**
  This software calculates eighteen different formulas presented with explanations and text analysis options. It will accept a text sample of any size.

- **Juicy Studio website (*http://juicystudio.com/services/readability.php*).**
  This website offers calculations using three readability formulas and has an input option that is specific to the readability of websites.

- **OKAPI! Website (*http://www.interventioncentral.org/htmdocs/tools/okapi/okapi.shtml*).**
  This website offers a readability calculator for both Spache and Dale-Chall. The user can choose to calculate the readability of materials of up to 170 words. The program will highlight the "hard words" not found on the word frequency lists used in the formulas.

- **Online-Utility.org (*www.online-utility.org/english/readability_test_and_improve.jsp*).**
  This international website offers six calculations based on accepted formulas and offers suggestions for easing the readability of the entered text.

websites. Title listings simply report titles and reading levels of the materials. Micro Power and Light Co. markets a relatively inexpensive software package called Readability Calculations that can calculate the readability of any document using nine different formulas, including those reviewed here (*www.micropowerandlight.com*). The Intervention Central website also provides readability calculators (*www.interventioncentral. org*).

## A Brief Comparison of Readability Formulas

Figure 2.5 contains Harrison's (1980) analysis of the validity, accuracy, and convenience of four of the five formulas discussed here. The Fry graph and the Flesch–Kincaid Grade Level have similar levels of validity and accuracy but the Fry is easier to apply. The Spache formula is quite valid but not quite as accurate as the Fry and the Flesch–Kincaid at age 8 (grade 3). The Dale–Chall formula trumps all in validity and accuracy at grade 3 and higher but is not as convenient. When convenience is an issue, either the Fry or the Flesch will suffice for upper elementary materials because they are highly correlated. Both the Spache and the Primary Readability formulas work best for materials at grades 1 and 2, but the latter has a more recent word list. Table 2.3 compares formula results for a list of common books. Overall, you can see that readability formulas rarely agree with each other exactly. You will get different results depending on the formula used. Specific results tend to differ most at the primary grades, where readability formulas are inherently limited (see Advantages and Disadvantages sections). These comparisons confirm that formulas only provide estimates.

| | Validity | Age level accuracy (8–16 age range) | Ease of application |
|---|---|---|---|
| Flesch formula (Grade score) | •••• | ••• | •• |
| Fry graph | •••• | ••• | ••• |
| Powers–Sumner–Kearl formula | •••• | • | ••• |
| Mugford formula and chart | •••• | •••• | •• |
| FOG formula | ••• | •• | •••• |
| SMOG formula | ••• | •• | ••••• |
| Dale–Chall formula | ••••• | •••• | • |
| Spache formula | •••• | •• | •• |
| FORCAST formula | •• | •• | •••• |

*Note.* The greater the number of indicators (•), the better the performance of the tool. The Powers et al., FOG, SMOG, and FORCAST formulas are not reviewed in the book.

**FIGURE 2.5.** A comparison of the validity, accuracy, and ease of application for readability formulas. From Harrison (1980). Copyright 1980 by Cambridge University Press. Reprinted by permission.

**TABLE 2.3. A Comparison of the Reading Levels Delivered by Five Common Readability Formulas**

| Grade | Sample text | New Dale–Chall | Fry | Flesch–Kincaid Grade level | Spache | Primary | M |
|-------|-------------|---------------|-----|------------------------|--------|---------|---|
| 1 | Frog and Toad Together | 1 | 2 | 1.8 | 2.4 | 1.5 | 1.7 |
| 2 | A Bargain for Francis | 2 | 2 | 1.8 | 2.4 | 2 | 2.0 |
| 3 | The Boxcar Children: Mystery Behind the Wall | 3 | 4 | 3.6 | 3.3 | 3 | 3.4 |
| 4 | The Indian in the Cupboard | 4 | 3 | 5.7 | NA[a] | 5 | 4.4 |
| 5 | The TV Kid | 5–6[b] | 5 | 5.4 | NA[a] | 5 | 5.2 |

[a]Spache levels end at 3.9.
[b]5.5 used in calculating the mean.

## GUIDELINES FOR USING READABILITY FORMULAS

If readability expert Klare (1963) were to continue his review of research on formulas today, he might have called the era beginning in the 1990s the Technology Era. Hand-calculating readability using formulas is a thing of the past. Karen, a teacher described in Chapter 7, uses an online catalogue with readability formulas to find materials for her students. Although many teachers still rely on the five common formulas discussed here, they access results using online readability calculators or software. However, the new, speedier applications have not eradicated potential misuses. Readability formulas have both advantages and disadvantages (Table 2.4).

### Advantages

Most teachers need a streamlined tool for managing many different readers with many different texts. Formulas give teachers a place to start because even the most widely read educators would find it impossible to assess every book their students want to read. The greatest advantage of readability formulas is that they provide approximate levels of difficulty of many books in a time- and effort-efficient manner. As Rhonda, a third-grade teacher, remarked to me, "You know sometimes success in teaching is about logistics. . . . handling the needs of many different people efficiently." Rhonda's point highlights the major strength of readability formulas: They are pragmatic. Despite the criticisms, readability formulas are still in use today because they fill a need.

**TABLE 2.4. Advantages and Disadvantages of Readability Formulas**

| Advantages | Disadvantages |
|---|---|
| Formulas provide *time- and energy-efficient* ways to obtain basic information about text difficulty for initially matching readers to texts. | Formulas *do not account for many important factors in text–reader matching* like text content, text layout, print features (font, spacing). |
| Formulas are *objective and reliable*, delivering the same estimates no matter who applies the formula. | The grade-level estimates are *not as precise* as they seem. They can be off by one-half to one whole grade level. |
| Formulas have a deep *history of research* exposing both the pros and cons of formulas. | Formulas are not sensitive enough for readers *at the earliest stages of reading (preprimer, primer, early first).* |

The second advantage of the readability formulas is that they are objective and reliable. Within a particular formula, results are usually quite consistent. Thus, formulas help teachers and researchers compare many different texts. A science curriculum committee, of which I was a member, used readability formulas to estimate the difficulties of the print materials in each curricula being reviewed. We found that some publishers had materials that were consistently more difficult than others. Also, the passages in some publishers' curriculum were quite irregular, with one passage being very easy and another being quite difficult. (As detailed later in the General Considerations section, careful analysis of other text features is very important in reviewing content area materials as well.) Similarly, teachers can use readability formulas to determine whether difficulty levels in stories in a basal reading text are consistent throughout. When teachers are selecting books for literature study, they often need to know about how difficult their collection is.

The last advantage of readability formulas is that they have a rich history. Readability formulas have been well studied and researched, unlike some of the newer tools. I believe that the research on readability over the years has strengthened the formulas.

## Disadvantages

Readability formulas, like software or teacher's manuals, are tools, and they have limitations. Readability formulas do not account for many important factors in matching texts with readers, among them readers' interests, background knowledge, content, or motivation. I remember finding a book on *Native Americans* for Kyle, a boy who was very interested in nonfiction. Throughout the book, the author used the term *Native American*. At the end of the book, Kyle turned to me and said, "This book isn't about Americans. It is about people in different countries. Where is Cherokee, anyway?" Kyle was missing some fundamental information about the term Native American and the history of our country that prevented him from truly understanding the passage. The readability formula had failed to account for Kyle's knowledge about the topic of the text.

The second disadvantage is that the grade-level estimates can vary. Depending on the formula, the standard error can be one-half to 1 year. When formulas are compared, as in Table 2.3, they are usually, but not always, within one grade level. Occasionally, formulas vary up to two grade levels. The point is that grade-level estimates are not always as exact as they sound. Estimates, therefore, should be treated as ballpark figures.

The third disadvantage is that formulas are often not sensitive enough for beginning readers. Developers designed readability formulas to give broad reading levels (e.g., grade 1, grade 2, and grade 3), and the broad levels simply do not parse text difficulty into the small increments that beginning readers need. Most readability formulas do not give a level below grade 1 even though beginning readers spend a great deal of time reading materials that are at the preprimer and primer levels. As detailed in Chapter 4, beginning readers need the support of text features not measured by formulas, such as decodability, repetition and pacing, formatting, and illustrations. The second problem with using readability formulas on beginning reading materials is that the texts do not contain enough words to meet required sample lengths. The Fry graph, for example, requires three 100-word samples, but many beginning reading texts do not even contain one 100-word sample. When the sample length is reduced, additional error is introduced into the formula. Some developers have addressed this issue by giving procedures to use with smaller samples but problems still exist.

## General Considerations

Readability formulas do not select books. They do not make professional judgments. Readability formulas are only tools. Teachers use readability formulas to find books for students, and they need some guidelines for this process. Table 2.5 details guidelines for using readability formulas. The rule of thumb is to know the goodness of fit (i.e., how well the formula will serve your purposes in working with students at your grade level). The second rule of thumb is to use the readability formulas in concert with other information about the text and the

## TABLE 2.5. Guidelines for Using Readability Formulas

| Guideline | How to apply the guideline |
|---|---|
| Know the formula. | To prevent misuse, users should know the following about formulas:<br>• Its goodness of fit: At what levels or grade ranges does the formula *best* estimate difficulty?<br>• The level for which the formula was originally designed (adults, primary students, elementary students).<br>• The units used: whole grades or whole grades and tenths?<br>• The criterion used to create the formula (other formula results, student test performance, teacher ratings, information student performance). |
| Use readability formulas with other subjective information. | All of the major readability researchers acknowledge that formulas should be used in conjunction with other information such as<br>• Text content.<br>• Text organization, layout, print features (font, spacing).<br>• Reading context (how much support the reader will be receiving).<br>• Reader factors (abilities, motivation, knowledge). |
| Be aware of the ways vocabulary-based formulas can underestimate difficulty. | If materials have any of the following, then a vocabulary-based formula can *underestimate* difficulty:<br>• Common words with lesser known meanings (e.g., *The lion pants*).<br>• Metaphorical language (e.g., *She was sunny*).<br>• Idioms (e.g., *Get the bugs out*).<br>• Archaic uses (e.g., *The gentleman came to call*).<br>• Unusual sentence structures (e.g., *To the wood he would go*). |
| Be aware of the ways that formulas can over- and underestimate difficulty of science and social text materials. | If unusual, technical words are frequently repeated in the text, then formula results may *overestimate* difficulty.<br>• If unusual, technical words are clearly explained or illustrated, then formula results may *overestimate* difficulty.<br>• If the passage has a *high concept load* and introduces many different concepts within a short passage, then the formula may *underestimate* difficulty. |
| With adapted materials, be alert for formula-conforming changes that may actually make texts more difficult. | Basal collections, high-interest/low-readability materials, and materials written for struggling readers may have been adapted. Although useful, review these materials carefully for the alterations listed in Table 2.1:<br>• Missing connections<br>• Shifted topic and focus<br>• Deleted information<br>• Shifted point of view<br>• Replaced vocabulary |
| Use readability formulas with connected prose. | Do not apply formulas to any of the following:<br>• Poetry<br>• Recipes<br>• Song lyrics/raps<br>• Worksheets<br>• Mathematical formulas |

reader. From the perspective of most formula developers, the process of text–reader matching does not stop with formula results. In fact, Chall and Dale (1995) and Gunning (2003) both provided checklists for teachers so that they may address additional factors in matching that are not covered with readability formulas. Gunning's checklist guides users to consider the support of illustrations, the difficulty of the concepts, difficulty of letters and sounds, and degree of repetition. The checklists address reader factors such as ability, background knowledge, and interest. In *Qualitative Assessment of Text Difficulty*, Chall et al. (1996) provided sample passages of six different text types in grades 1 to 16. These anchor passages give teachers a feel for the kind of writing that typifies literature and nonfiction at different grade levels.

As with many tools that work with normally developing readers, readability formulas may require some tweaking when the target population includes struggling readers, learning-disabled readers, or English language learners. When readers have little or no background knowledge, readability formula results may underestimate the difficulty of the material for them, particularly for English language learners. I remember mistakenly choosing a book with a Halloween theme for a Korean student, with no background knowledge about the holiday. While technically an appropriate choice, the student's background knowledge made it less readable.

Additionally, vocabulary-based formulas can underestimate difficulty. Sometimes common words can be used in uncommon ways, rendering them more difficult than assumed by the formulas (Venable, 2003). As detailed in Table 2.5, formulas will not take into account metaphorical language, idioms, and archaic usage. When using materials containing these elements, the formula results will *underestimate* text difficulty.

As discussed earlier, similar issues arise with science and social studies texts, in which formulas can overestimate the difficulty. Results on content texts will be inflated if technical terms are repeated and supported by clear explanations and illustrations. However, the grade-level estimates will not be inflated if the material has a number of difficult words that are not repeated or well described. Some content area materials carry a high concept load, meaning that they introduce more difficult words and repeat them less. Some science textbooks will introduce several novel concepts in a short space. In one 125-word passage that I reviewed, a science text introduced the following terms: *solutions, mixtures, homogeneous, heterogeneous, solutes,* and *suspensions.* For the average third grader, most of these terms are new, and a passage that introduces them so abruptly has a high concept load. In content area materials, a review for repetition, writing style, clarity, concept load, and support will elucidate the validity of a grade-level estimate.

Readability formulas will not work with certain types of material. For example, poetry, which often lacks ending punctuation, will yield odd formula results. The same is true of mathematical material. Primary historical documents, now widely used in history classes, are not suited to using formulas. Finally, most of the traditional formulas and many of the enhanced formulas were not designed to be used with websites. Websites are a unique blend of text, layout, pictures, photographs, and links. Although I have seen readability calculators for websites, I believe that assessing their readability is far more complicated than applying a formula using word- and sentence-level variables.

The reading context is a final component that teachers should consider as they use readability formulas. Students read in many different situations, including independent, small-group, and large-group assignments; recreationally; content learning; test taking; online reading; and task performance. Use of formula results should coordinate with the reading context. In the Randall and Carol White Reading and Math Center at Oklahoma State University, we use a scale to describe the level of support that will be present in a given situation, ranging from no support, to at-home and in-school sustained silent reading, large-group and small-group support, and one-on-one support. When we help the students choose materials for their take-home backpacks, we will assume no support and identify materials that are at least one-half to one grade level below the student's instructional level. Figure 2.6 illustrates that, as difficulty increases, greater levels of support are needed until the material is frustrational and no level of support would help the reader. We emphasize that even within the students' instructional range, different contexts can influence text choices. For instance, one-on-one teaching contexts allow the selection of more difficult materials in the student's instructional range than whole-group teaching contexts do. If we want students to read in a large-group instructional setting, then materials cannot be as difficult because large-group settings are less supportive.

## SUMMARY

The major strength of readability formulas—objectivity—is also a major weakness. Although readability formulas provide statistically strong and reliable estimates, they will not address stylistic elements, word usage, and other subjective elements. The advantages of readability formulas include their strong statistical properties and the ease with which they

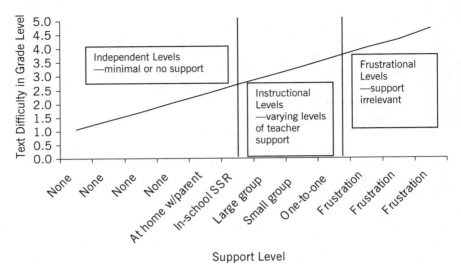

**FIGURE 2.6.** The relationship between text difficulty and levels of support (SSR, sustained silent reading).

can be applied using software applications. They are time efficient and give teachers a place to start with students. However, readability formulas only begin the process of matching texts and readers. They have limited use with beginning readers, do not represent content, and have flaws that either can over- or underestimate difficulty. As tools for text analysis, readability formulas do what they were designed to do: estimate text difficulty.

# CHAPTER 3

# Second-Generation Readability Formulas

## Lexiles and Degrees of Reading Power

Everything new was old once.
    —UNATTRIBUTED

Several years ago, I saw a newspaper article entitled "New Framework Takes the Guesswork Out of Finding Books for Readers." Next to the article was a photo of smiling third graders holding up novels. The article was about the Lexile Framework, and I found it quite funny because the Lexile Framework is really something old becoming new again. In fact, as Chall and Dale (1995) explained, "At the height of criticism of classic readability [1988], Lexile Theory, a classic readability measure, was published" (p. 89). Both Lexiles and Degrees of Reading Power (DRP) are second-generation readability formulas. They were built upon the same principles as traditional readability formulas like the Fry, Flesch–Kincaid, Spache, and Dale–Chall (see Chapter 2), but they are advanced in some fundamental ways. Both have harnessed technology to support formulas, with comprehensive word lists numbering in the millions. Both have used technology to sample substantive portions of texts. Both provide parallel reader and text measures that allow users to obtain a reader's level and a text's difficulty in equivalent units. Both have units other than grade levels to express text difficulty. These enhanced tools have added precision and power to traditional readability theory.

Lexiles and DRP are gaining in popularity. At least 15 states, including Texas, California, North Carolina, and Georgia, have Lexile leveled their state tests, meaning that teachers in these states have access to their students' reading levels in Lexiles. In addition, Scholastic Publishing Company provides Lexile levels on many of its books and sells Lexile Leveled Libraries to its customers. DRP provides difficulty ratings for hundreds of textbooks, and many school districts across the country use its tests. Testing companies also use these enhanced formulas to measure passages on standardized tests and to equate test forms. Yet, even as these tools are gaining ground, they are not receiving adequate attention in the professional literature. At a minimum, schools and teachers need to understand the underpinnings of Lexiles and DRP and how these unusual units translate into grade levels. The overview of readability formulas in Chapter 2 lays the groundwork for this chapter because Lexiles and DRP are grounded in classic readability.

This chapter summarizes the features and uses of the Lexile Framework and DRP. The first section provides a brief overview of second-generation readability formulas, describing specifically how they represent a separate, advanced class of text analysis tools. The subsequent sections describe the two tools and review existing research. Grade-level conversions, Lexile-leveled assessments, and sample DRP test items provide important information for choosing and using these tools. The final section provides guidelines for using Lexiles and DRP.

## OVERVIEW OF SECOND-GENERATION READABILITY FORMULAS

Many experienced teachers and reading specialists do not realize that these second-generation formulas are the offspring of formulas they know. The second-generation formulas possess three features that distinguish them from their predecessors. First, research companies created and own the rights to these formulas. A company called MetaMetrics, Inc. designed the Lexile framework in 1984 in response to a contract issued by the National Institute of Child Health and Human Development (NICHD). NICHD wanted a tool to analyze the difficulty of passages used in the National Assessment of Educational Progress. The Lexile Framework and its copyrights are now owned by MetaMetrics, which makes the framework commercially available to consumers. DRP was created in 1976 by a company called Touchstone Applied Science and Associates, Inc. (TASA). The State of New York contracted the company to design measures for students and standards for texts that would assist the state in tracking student performance and matching texts with readers. The property rights for the DRP products are now owned by Questar Assessment and also made available to consumers. Because the formulas are proprietary, they are not publicly available for scrutiny and independent research. They have not been the subject of peer-reviewed research to the degree that traditional readability formulas were. The proprietary nature of these formulas often limits information about them to white papers and reports published by the companies. In fact, MetaMetrics publishes its own journal, *Popular Measurement*.

The second unique characteristic of these formulas is that they use distinctive units to express text difficulty. Whereas traditional formulas use grade levels, both Lexiles and DRP have their own unique units. The Lexile Framework uses Lexiles, numbering in the hundreds, and DRP uses Degrees of Reading Power, numbering in the tens. These unique units permit text difficulty to be divided into many different levels that are free of the stigma of grade levels. In addition, these units are calibrated and represent equal intervals of difficulty (Chall & Dale, 1995). As discussed later, the unique units have both advantages and disadvantages depending on the purpose.

Third, all of these formulas provide parallel text and reader forms. The Lexile Framework and DRP both have tests in which readers' levels can be obtained in Lexiles or DRP. With the difficulty level of texts also available in DRP and Lexiles, matching readers with texts can be theoretically more precise. When teachers use parallel forms to make a match, they do not introduce additional error that comes from using a different tool to assess student reading levels.

## LEXILES

### Text Features

Lexiles are nothing more than units of measure, just like miles, seconds, inches, or degrees Fahrenheit, but they measure units of text difficulty as opposed to distance, time, or temperature. In purpose, Lexile units are analogous to grade levels because they express text difficulty. However, Lexiles offer many more steps than traditional readability formulas, which may assign only a single grade level or a grade and tenths to a book (e.g., 2.1, 2.2, 2.3, 2.4, 2.5, 2.6). Text difficulty in Lexile units ranges from 200 to 1700L (Lennon & Burdick, 2004). Because Lexiles break text difficulty into hundreds of steps, as opposed to single grade levels, the tool is theoretically more exact. Lexiles are like teaspoons, whereas grade levels are cups. Table 3.1 translates Lexiles into grade lev-

**TABLE 3.1. Translation of Lexiles to Grade Levels to Degrees of Reading Power (DRP)**

| Grade | Lexile text measures | DRP |
|-------|---------------------|------|
| 1 | 200–400 | 40–43 |
| 2 | 300–500 | 44–47 |
| 3 | 500–700 | 48–49 |
| 4 | 650–850 | 50–51 |
| 5 | 750–950 | 52–53 |
| 6 | 850–1050 | 54–55 |
| 7 | 950–1075 | 56–57 |
| 8 | 1000–1100 | 58–59 |
| 9 | 1050–1150 | 60–61 |
| 10 | 1100–1200 | 62–63 |
| 11–12 | 1100–1300 | 63–65 |

Note. Data from *www.lexile.com* and Gunning (2003).

els. Typically, each grade level spans about 200L. Second grade, for example, runs from about 300 to 500L. The range of difficulty includes 200 levels of difficulty as opposed to the 10 typical of traditional readability formulas. Because children in different grades will read at a range of levels, there is overlap in the Lexile ranges for each grade. The General Considerations section discusses scenarios in which this degree of specificity might be helpful.

Like classic readability formulas, there are two major aspects of the Lexile text analysis: word difficulty and sentence difficulty. With a nod to classic readability formulas, the Lexile framework estimates word difficulty through word frequency. Chapter 2 discussed the relationship between frequency and difficulty: More frequently occurring words are usually more familiar to readers than less frequently occurring words. However, word frequency is not a perfect estimate of difficulty. To improve readability estimates, the Lexile system decreases sampling error by increasing the size of the word base (corpus) on which estimates are based (Kamil, 2004). Before the Lexile formula was established, readability estimates were based on lists no larger than about 5 million words. Now, as a result of computer technology, frequencies are based on a sample of 600 million words taken from 37,000 books (Lennon & Burdick, 2004). MetaMetrics analyzes texts using a sampling process called "slicing" (Lennon & Burdick, 2004). It estimates sentence difficulty by counting the number of words in each sentence and using the mean sentence length for all slices of the text in a book. Slices of about 125 words are analyzed at a time and the results for each slice are averaged across the book. Note that the traditional formulas rely on no more than 400-word *samples* from each text. The Lexile sampling process is more thorough. Just like traditional formulas, the Lexile Framework should be applied to continuous text passages that contain standard punctuation. Poems, lists, recipes, and song lyrics are not analyzed because they do not have conventional punctuation (Lennon & Burdick, 2004). When analyzing these types of materials, Lexile software will read the prose as one sentence, thereby skewing the results significantly. Figure 3.1 summarizes the text features in both Lexiles and DRP.

MetaMetrics makes available the Lexile levels of books free of charge at the company's website (*www.lexile.com*). More than 100,000 titles are available, and the database is searchable by title, author, keywords, Lexile range, and ISBN. This database is available for purchase on a CD, which enables the user to print Lexile labels. More than 100 publishers have their books Lexile leveled. The Lexile Framework Reading Map, available for purchase, lists well-known titles at different Lexile levels. Table 3.2 contains the Lexile levels of a list of popular books. (For comparative purposes, the DRP for similar titles is available in Figure 3.2.)

**Easiest Books**
*Frequently occurring words*
*Short sentences*

**More Difficult Books**
*Less frequently occurring words*
*Longer sentences*

| Text feature | How the feature is estimated | |
| --- | --- | --- |
| | **Lexiles** | **Degrees of Reading Power** |
| **Semantic Difficulty** *Word difficulty* | Word Frequency (mean log frequency) | Number of words not on the Dale–Chall (1995) list of 3,000 words known to 80% of 4th graders AND Number of letters per word |
| **Syntactic Difficulty** *Sentence difficulty* | Mean Sentence Length (number of words) | Number of words per sentence |

**FIGURE 3.1.** A summary of the basis of Lexile and DRP units.

MetaMetrics uses several codes in analyzing texts. These five categories include nonconforming (NC) text, illustrated glossary (IG), beginning reading (BR) text, nonprose (NP) text, and adult-directed (AD) text. NC text has content that is appropriate for a younger child but a difficulty that is higher. An IG is a book that contains independent pieces of text such as an encyclopedia. A BR text is one that, when analyzed, has a Lexile score of 0 or below. These are books that are very simple, like the leveled texts described in Chapter 6. The book *Houses and*

**TABLE 3.2. A List of Common Titles with Lexile Levels**

| Lexile level | Title |
| --- | --- |
| 1510 | *The Prince* |
| 1420 | *The Scarlet Letter* |
| 1410 | *Profiles in Courage* |
| 1410 | *One Hundred Years of Solitude* |
| 1390 | *Moll Flanders* |
| 1340 | *Silent Spring* |
| 1330 | *Roots* |
| 1310 | *Democracy in America* |
| 1170 | *Animal Farm* |
| 1100 | *Across Five Aprils* |
| 1080 | *Anne Frank: The Diary of a Young Girl* |
| 1070 | *Robinson Crusoe* |
| 1000 | *The Hobbit* |
| 1000 | *Island of the Blue Dolphins* |
| 910 | *Old Yeller* |
| 890 | *Jane Eyre* |
| 880 | *Harry Potter and the Sorcerer's Stone* |
| 750 | *The Adventures of Tom Sawyer* |
| 680 | *Charlotte's Web* |
| 670 | *Number the Stars* |
| 650 | *How to Eat Fried Worms* |
| 560 | *Sarah, Plain and Tall* |
| 560 | *Math Curse* |
| 560 | *Superfudge* |
| 530 | *Chicka Chicka Boom Boom* |
| 490 | *The Boxcar Children* |
| 400 | *Frog and Toad Are Friends* |
| 330 | *Shoeshine Girl* |
| 260 | *The Cat in the Hat* |
| 220 | *Clifford, the Big Red Dog* |
| 210 | *The Golly Sisters Go West* |
| 140 | *Amelia Bedelia* |
| 130 | *Nate the Great* |
| 130 | *Morris the Moose* |
| 3 | *Green Eggs and Ham* |
| BR | *Are You My Mother?* |

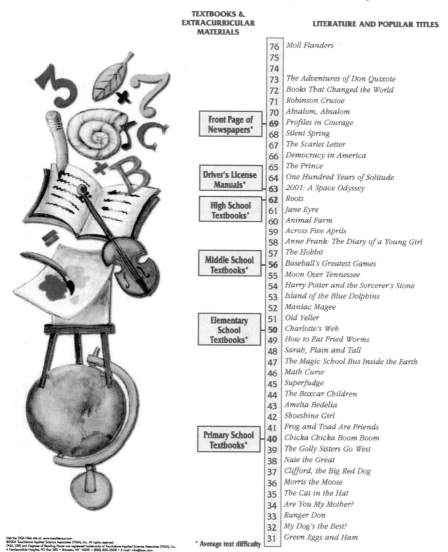

| TEXTBOOKS & EXTRACURRICULAR MATERIALS | | LITERATURE AND POPULAR TITLES |
|---|---|---|
| | 76 | Moll Flanders |
| | 75 | |
| | 74 | |
| | 73 | The Adventures of Don Quixote |
| | 72 | Books That Changed the World |
| | 71 | Robinson Crusoe |
| Front Page of Newspapers* | 70 | Absalom, Absalom |
| | 69 | Profiles in Courage |
| | 68 | Silent Spring |
| | 67 | The Scarlet Letter |
| | 66 | Democracy in America |
| | 65 | The Prince |
| Driver's License Manuals* | 64 | One Hundred Years of Solitude |
| | 63 | 2001: A Space Odyssey |
| High School Textbooks* | 62 | Roots |
| | 61 | Jane Eyre |
| | 60 | Animal Farm |
| | 59 | Across Five Aprils |
| | 58 | Anne Frank: The Diary of a Young Girl |
| Middle School Textbooks* | 57 | The Hobbit |
| | 56 | Baseball's Greatest Games |
| | 55 | Moon Over Tennessee |
| | 54 | Harry Potter and the Sorcerer's Stone |
| | 53 | Island of the Blue Dolphins |
| | 52 | Maniac Magee |
| Elementary School Textbooks* | 51 | Old Yeller |
| | 50 | Charlotte's Web |
| | 49 | How to Eat Fried Worms |
| | 48 | Sarah, Plain and Tall |
| | 47 | The Magic School Bus Inside the Earth |
| | 46 | Math Curse |
| | 45 | Superfudge |
| | 44 | The Boxcar Children |
| | 43 | Amelia Bedelia |
| | 42 | Shoeshine Girl |
| Primary School Textbooks* | 41 | Frog and Toad Are Friends |
| | 40 | Chicka Chicka Boom Boom |
| | 39 | The Golly Sisters Go West |
| | 38 | Nate the Great |
| | 37 | Clifford, the Big Red Dog |
| | 36 | Morris the Moose |
| | 35 | The Cat in the Hat |
| | 34 | Are You My Mother? |
| | 33 | Ranger Don |
| | 32 | My Dog's the Best! |
| | 31 | Green Eggs and Ham |

* Average text difficulty

**FIGURE 3.2.** DRP Scale of Text Difficulty. Copyright 2004 by Touchstone Applied Science Associates (TASA), Inc. Reprinted by permission.

*Homes*, written by Ann Morris in 1993, is an example of a BR book. AD texts are those that are usually not easily read by the age group for which they were designed and require adult support. For example, *Where the Wild Things Are* is an AD text with 740L. The story and themes are written for primary students, many of whom would have difficulty with some of the words in the book. NP is material that contains 50% or more text that is not prose, such as poems, raps, and plays.

## Readers' Lexile Levels

Before the second-generation formulas evolved, educators used different tools to assess text difficulty and readers. For example, a teacher might use an informal reading inventory (IRI) to estimate a student's reading level. Then the teacher might rely on one of the many readability formulas to estimate text difficulty. One problem with this approach is that the text measures estimate difficulty in grades and tenths but the instruments use whole grades. For example, the Analytical Reading Inventory (Woods & Moe, 2006) might indicate that Dion reads instructionally at the third-grade level, and the Spache readability formula would estimate text difficulty to the nearest tenth of a grade (i.e., 3.1, 3.2, 3.4). Unfortunately, the teacher is left to decide whether Dion would be best matched to 3.1 books or 3.9 books. The second issue is that the text measure and the reader measure have no relationship to each other and may define third-grade material in slightly different ways using different readability formulas.

MetaMetrics solves this problem by using parallel tests and text measures. The Lexile level for a student is a targeted level at which he can comprehend 75% of the material. The Lexile Framework is instrument independent and can be applied to any test. The box on p. 51 lists a number of common standardized tests that provide reader Lexile levels. As mentioned earlier, a number of states are also Lexile leveling their criterion-referenced tests. The most up-to-date information about states that have Lexile-leveled tests is available at the Lexiles website (*www.lexile.com*): Click Partners/Resources/Assessments and Reading Programs. When students take a test using Lexile-leveled text, the results will provide their reading levels in Lexiles. The Lexile level is the point at which a student can read and comprehend about 75% of the text. A 75% comprehension level typically corresponds with instructional-level materials (Harrison, 1980). MetaMetrics does not, however, use the term "instructional level." It states that the Lexile level is the level at which students will be challenged but not frustrated. The test will also include the student's Lexile range, which is ± 50 to 100 points.

# COMMON ASSESSMENTS
## THAT PROVIDE STUDENT LEXILE LEVELS

- **Gates–MacGinitie Reading Test (GMRT-4)**
  Publisher:                  Riverside Publishing Company
  Type of assessment:         Standardized
  Other:                      Book list provided

- **Iowa Test of Basic Skills (ITBS and ITED)**
  Publisher:                  Riverside Publishing Company
  Type of assessment:         Standardized
  Other:                      Book list provided

- **Metropolitan Achievement Test (MAT-8)**
  Publisher:                  Harcourt Assessment
  Type of assessment:         Standardized

- **Scholastic Reading Inventory (SRI) and SRI Interactive (computer based)**
  Publisher:                  Scholastic
  Type of assessment:         Informal reading inventory
  Other:                      Paper–pencil and computerized

- **Stanford Diagnostic Achievement Test 9 and 10 (SAT-9/SAT-10)**
  Publisher:                  Harcourt Assessment
  Type of assessment:         Standardized

- **Stanford Diagnostic Reading Test (SDRT-4)**
  Publisher:                  Harcourt Assessment
  Type of assessment:         Standardized

- **TerraNova Assessment Series (CAT/6, CTBS/5)**
  Publisher:                  CTB/McGraw-Hill
  Type of assessment:         Standardized

- **State Assessments:**
  States reporting Lexile levels:   Texas, North Carolina, California, Georgia

A number of standardized assessments and some informal assessments have been Lexile leveled. Having parallel text and student measures does take some guesswork out of matching, but tests still have error, and readability formulas do not account for all the factors that make texts difficult.

### Research on Lexiles

Existing research on the Lexile Framework comes in two forms: that which has been performed by MetaMetrics and that which has not. Research performed by MetaMetrics will promote the interests of the company, whereas research performed independently has no obligation to do so. Over the 20 years of developing the Lexile Framework, MetaMetrics has been praised by reading experts (Chall & Dale, 1995; Hall & Moats, 1998; Kamil, 2004; White & Clements, 2001). The framework is valid. It does what it is supposed to do: determine the difficulty of passages in ways that connect with actual performance on standardized tests (Smith, Stenner, Horabin, & Smith, 1989; Walpole, Hayes, & Robnolt, 1989). In addition, it is reliable, consistently predicting passage difficulty and student level. Basically, the Lexile Framework has excellent psychometric properties.

Independent research on the Lexile Framework is sparse. Lexile levels correlate with nine readability formulas (Chall & Dale, 1995). Walpole et al. (2006) examined the relationship between Lexile levels obtained through the Scholastic Reading Inventory (SRI) and the accuracy and fluency with which second graders read materials at their Lexile levels. The results showed that 43 of 46 readers read books at their Lexile levels with 90% or more accuracy, indicating that Lexiles matched readers to texts 93% of the time. However, the SRI and Lexile levels did not reflect books that students could read fluently. About 43% of the sample read books at their Lexile levels below 71 words per minute, a basic standard for second grade. Thus, Lexile scores and book levels may not help teachers in finding books that can be read fluently.

## DEGREES OF READING POWER

### Text Features

Like Lexiles, DRPs are unique units to express text difficulty. Texts range from about 15 to 85 DRP. Questar Assessment elected to use DRP as opposed to grade levels because students in a given grade will vary in their actual reading levels, and grade levels tend to shift as expectations in schools change and grow. Second graders will read at the first-, second-, third-, and fourth-grade levels. We expect second graders to have different competencies in 2007 than they did 20 years ago. DRPs do not carry the loaded messages that grade levels do, a criticism of traditional readability formulas. Table 3.1 translates DRP to grade levels and Lexiles. Note that a grade level covers between 2 and 3 DRP. Figure 3.2 shows the DRP of a number of common materials. Typical first-grade materials like *Clifford, the Big Red Dog* and *The Cat in the Hat* have DRP levels in the 30s. *Charlotte's Web*, a typical third-grade book, has a DRP of 50; *Harry Potter and the Sorcerer's Stone*, a DRP of 54; and *Jane Eyre*, a material appropriate in late high school or college, a DRP of 61.

Unlike Lexiles, DRP units have a narrower range. A 1-unit increase in DRP is more meaningful. In DRPs *Charlotte's Web* and *Harry Potter and the Sorcerer's Stone* differ by 4 units but in Lexiles they differ by 200 units (*Charlotte's Web*, 680L; *Harry Potter*, 880L). In this example, 1 DRP appears to be approximately equal to 50L. Figure 3.2 also indicates some disagreements between Lexile levels and DRPs. These may be accounted for by the different word-level estimates and sampling procedures. However, DRPs and Lexile levels in this set of titles were highly correlated by my analysis ($r = .95$, $p < .01$).

The quote at the beginning of this chapter that refers to the new being old reflects DRP exactly. The new DRP almost replicates the old Bormuth cloze mean formula (Bormuth, 1971). See the box on p. 54 for a description of cloze procedures. In fact, the text features used in DRP come directly from Bormuth's formula, and the reader measure is a cloze passage. DRP uses two word features: the number of letters per word and the number of words not on the Dale–Chall list of 3,000 words known to fourth graders. This is the same Dale–Chall list used in the new Dale–Chall formula described in Chapter 2. To estimate sentence difficulty, DRP uses average number of words per sentence. Figure 3.1 summarizes DRP text features.

Questar Assessment offers several tools for obtaining the DRPs for books, among them the DRP Booklink Software, which contains the difficulty of 33,000 fiction and nonfiction titles. For each book, the list gives the title, author, publisher, page count, and ISBN. This list is searchable by title and category and, unlike the Lexile list, has annotations. Teachers can create lists of titles for students based on level and interest. Sample booklists are viewable at the Questar Assessment website (*www.questarai.com*). Questar Assessment also has a searchable database on the website with the DRP of textbooks. At a cost, Questar Assessment will also provide readability analysis of books not on the DRP Booklink Software for publishers, librarians, and DRP school systems.

## A BRIEF DESCRIPTION OF CLOZE PROCEDURES

Cloze tests were proposed in 1953 by Taylor. Cloze passages are deletion tests. Test developers delete every fifth word from a passage and readers are asked to accurately guess the word that belongs in each blank. The readers' rate of accuracy in filling in the blanks estimates the text difficulty. Accuracy rate is based on readers identifying the exact word omitted from the passage. For instance, if the word "angry" was omitted from the text, then the word "mad," would be unacceptable. Cloze procedures rely on verbatim responses because they are usually more reliable, require less judgment, and take less time to score (Harrison, 1980).

If readers accurately fill in 40 to 45% of blanks in a passage, then it is considered an instructional passage (Bormuth, 1971). If accuracy is at about 57 to 61%, then the material is independent; if the score is less than 40%, then the material is frustrational. These percentages seem quite low. However, they attest to the difficulty of accurately predicting words without any graphic information about the word.

According to Harrison (1980), *cloze* refers to gestalt psychologists who suggested that the mind has propensity to complete or bring closure to incomplete figures. In a cloze test, the reader is completing a passage. Proponents of cloze testing note that the passages directly measure the difficulty of passages, as opposed to the difficulty of questions, and estimate the knowledge the reader brings to the task. Critics of cloze testing suggest that the measures actually estimate the degree of information in a passage that would help a person fill in a word, the passage redundancy. For instance, in the following passage, the repetition of the word "loved" helps the reader fill in blanks: "Lilly loved school. She _____ (loved) the pointy pencils. She loved the _____ (squeaky) chalk" (Henkes, 1996).

Modified cloze testing is still quite prevalent. A modified cloze test, like the DRP described in this chapter, provides answer choices to the reader instead of asking him or her to produce them. Answer choices are equal syntactically and similar semantically so that the word's part of speech does not cue the reader (See Figure 3.3 for a sample of a modified cloze passage.) Cloze testing is used in the Accelerated Reader STAR test used to estimate reading level and in the Reading Counts tests as well.

## Obtaining Readers' DRP Levels

Like the Lexile Framework, the DRP uses a parallel measure to assess reading levels. The DRP will measure a student's instructional and independent levels. Unlike Lexiles, which rely on a host of commercially produced standardized tests, DRP has its own tests, both paper and computer based. These tests are modified cloze passages in which words have been systematically omitted and the reader must accurately fill in the blank with the missing word.

In standard DRP passages, seven words are omitted from a 325-word passage and the reader must choose the correct word from five options (see Figure 3.3 for a sample standard DRP test). For the DRP test items, all of the answer choices are syntactically acceptable and fit within the sentence. To choose the correct word, the reader must consider previous sentences and context. For example, the first item in the sample passage in Figure 3.3 is the sentence "The _____ is a long

Many trucks move on the roads of America. They carry things people need. They carry things people want. Trucks carry food. They carry flowers. They carry logs. Trucks even carry houses. The____1____ is a long one. There are many kinds of trucks. Each one carries certain kinds of things.

1 a) street        b) list
   c) bridge       d) climb
          e) border

Some trucks look like boxes. They are closed on all sides. Rain cannot get in. The freight is____2____. These trucks carry clothes. They carry paper. They carry goods that must stay dry.

2 a) sold          b) weighed
   c) delayed      d) scattered
          e) protected

Some trucks carry animals. The sides are made of boards. There are spaces between the boards. Air can get in. The animals can ____3____. These trucks carry cows. They carry pigs. They carry chickens too.

3 a) wait          b) breathe
   c) work         d) perform
          e) stretch

Some trucks are just platforms on wheels. They haul heavy loads. Some carry steel. Others carry logs. The load is held down by chains. Logging trucks also have posts on the sides. The logs do not____4____. They stay in place.

4 a) roll          b) burn
   c) show         d) float
          e) matter

Other trucks are giant tanks. They carry things that pour. Some carry milk. Others carry water. Still others carry oil.

**FIGURE 3.3.** Sample passage from a Standard DRP test. Copyright 2004 by Touchstone Applied Science Associates (TASA), Inc. Reprinted by permission.

one." The choices, *street, list, bridge, climb,* and *border,* all fit this sentence grammatically and semantically. However, the context suggests that only the option *list,* is the accurate answer choice. DRP tests claim to measure the reader's process of comprehending as it takes place rather than his or her memory or interpretation of the passage after it has been read. The standard DRP tests surface-level comprehension that may be less dependent on background knowledge.

There are six standard DRP tests: levels 0, 2, 4, 6, 7, 8 with alternate forms (J and K). The alternate forms allow pre- and posttesting to track performance. The Questar Assessment website will give up-to-date information about the level at which tests should be administered. Certain levels of primary tests are suggested for grades 1 through 3, and different test levels are available for grades 3 through 12. The primary tests are not recommended for use until a student has command of decoding skills, generally not at the beginning of grade 1. Two advanced tests are also available with equivalent forms at each level for pre- and posttesting (T-2, U-2, T-4, U-4). Advanced DRP tests assess more complex skills and require test takers to answer questions conceptually by using answer choices in the form of phrases or sentences. Test booklets can be reused, and tests can be scored using a transparent overlay.

## Research on DRP

DRP, like Lexiles, does not have a great deal of independent research. Recently, researchers compared the eye movements of 10 adult readers reading DRP assessment passages with blanks and normal passages without blanks (Paulson & Henry, 2002). When readers read non-DRP passages without blank spaces, their eyes moved forward at normal rates and did not jump around the page. However, when readers read DRP passages with blank spaces, their eyes darted around the passage without fixating on certain words or entire chunks of text. To the researchers, these data seemed to suggest that the DRP tests did not measure the reading process but instead altered readers' normal processes of reading. However, the real criticism in the eye movement data is not of DRP but of cloze procedures, in general, which are used in many programs, including Accelerated Reader and the SRI.

Carver (1984, 1985a, 1985b) conducted several research studies in the 1980s. In the first, he rescaled the DRP text difficulty scores to grade levels and found them to be reliable and valid text estimates. At the lower levels, estimates were within one grade level, and at the upper grades, they were within two grade levels. In a second study, he examined the DRP tests and found inconsistencies between the DRP student ability units and DRP text difficulty units. The two did not match, but in 1990 these issues were remedied (Carver, 1990).

## GUIDELINES FOR USING
## SECOND-GENERATION READABILITY FORMULAS

Because of their roots in classic readability theory, Lexiles and DRP will possess the same advantages and disadvantages as traditional readability formulas. As with traditional formulas, they are efficient, objective, and reliable. Likewise, however, Lexiles and DRP do not account for all factors in text analysis like content, reader interest, print features (font style, spacing), or layout. When I discuss second-generation tools with my graduate students, they usually want to know why schools or teachers would use these second-generation formulas if they are fundamentally the same as the traditional readability formulas. This section presents the advantages and disadvantages *specific* to second-generation formulas and offers guidelines for the use of these formulas in schools.

### Advantages

Overall, both the Lexile Framework and the DRP tools have three advantages (Table 3.3). Chief among them is that these tools measure student reading levels and text difficulty using the same units. Lexiles and DRP avoid the problems of mixing measures described earlier in the

**TABLE 3.3. Advantages and Disadvantages of Second-Generation Formulas**

| Advantages | Disadvantages |
| --- | --- |
| *Parallel student and text measures* estimate student reading levels and text difficulty in the same units. | The *unique units and scale* are not easily interpretable to schools, teachers, and researchers who are more familiar with grade levels. |
| A *broad range of units* adds specificity to text analysis. | The systems *require specific assessments* to properly make a text–reader match and these assessments may be costly to schools. |
| Computer technology increases the *power, speed, and sampling* of text analysis, making it more thorough and efficient. | These tools are *not well suited to the needs of beginners* at the earliest stages of reading. |

discussion of Dion. For example, an IRI might establish an instructional level as the point at which a student can comprehend 60% of material, but a text measure might assume 70% comprehension as a criterion for calculating text difficulty. In addition, schools that are already using any of the Lexile-leveled tests already have their students' Lexile levels available.

Second, these tools have a broad range of units, and, theoretically, this adds greater precision to text analysis. The range gives more information about texts than traditional formulas. For example, second-grade Student A has a Lexile level of 300 and a range of 200 to 350. Second grade Student B has a Lexile level of 450 and a range of 400 to 500L. Student A is actually at the lower half of the second-grade level, dipping into grade 1, whereas Student B is actually at the upper half of the second-grade level. These two second-grade students are very different. The units also make these second-generation tools particularly applicable in test development and research when many different passages must be compared. The interval scales of Lexiles and DRP also make the tools useful in research because particular statistical tests require interval scales.

Last, Lexiles and DRP harness today's computer technology to increase the sampling, power, and precision of text analysis. By harnessing digital scanning, companies can process a large volume of text efficiently. A difficulty estimate based on more words in text is going to be a bit more trustworthy than an estimate based on a smaller sampling. The second-generation formulas have also advanced the power of traditional readability formulas. Before Lexiles, the most up-to-date word frequency list was based on 5 million words (Carroll, Davies, & Richman, 1971). Lexile's list is now based on a corpus of 600 million words. The ease of access to text difficulty on the web is another technological advantage. Developers have researched Lexiles and DRP extensively over 20 years, and the ventures have been well funded and reviewed by experts. The Lexiles Framework, for instance, is praised by National Reading Panel member Kamil (2004) for its use of an advanced statistical tool: Rasch modeling. (DRP uses the same procedure.)

## Disadvantages

Despite their strengths, these second-generation readability formulas are not perfect. First, from a purely logistical standpoint, users don't easily understand the units. Many teachers are not familiar with Lexiles or DRP, and the unusual units present problems in communicating with parents. A second-grade parent might better understand that her child is reading at a second-grade level but less likely to understand the meaning of 300 Lexiles. Teachers also may find that it takes some time to internalize the meanings of these units themselves. I still think of *Superfudge* by Judy Blume as being a third-grade book and not a 560L book.

The fact that second-generation formulas have parallel text and reader forms is an advantage but also a disadvantage. When schools and teachers appropriately use Lexiles or DRP, they will have student reading levels in Lexiles or DRP, and this requires specific assessments. The need for specific tests introduces substantial costs in terms of time and money. Schools can purchase published IRIs for about $50 per teacher or can use running records at no cost. However, the SRI, a computerized inventory offering Lexile levels, costs several thousand dollars. The cost for the DRP test is similar. Furthermore, many other Lexile-leveled tests are standardized, summative achievement tests that schools administer only once or twice a year. If the administration is in the Spring, teachers cannot obtain student Lexile levels in a timely fashion.

The third disadvantage is that neither Lexiles nor DRP are well suited to the needs of beginning readers. As mentioned in Chapter 2, when students learn to read, they need materials that go beyond readability formulas. Both companies acknowledge this weakness. The DRP materials explicitly state that the tests should not be used until students have mastered decoding. Books with a Lexile level below 0 are rated as BR, but the various BR books may actually range in difficulty for young readers. The rather imprecise BR designation is differentiated using other systems, like qualitative leveling.

Finally, like all measures, the second-generation formulas do have error in the text and reader assessments (White & Clements, 2001). The true Lexile level of a text can be 50 points below and 100 points above the obtained Lexile level, which seems to equate to at least one-half grade, an improvement over the usual whole-grade ranges in traditional formulas.

In several instances, strengths and weaknesses of these systems are like a double-edged sword, with advantages also having a connected disadvantage. Both Lexiles and DRP perfect text–reader matching by measuring reading levels and text levels in the same units. The parallel test and reader forms also can be a disadvantage because schools must use or purchase specific assessments to properly use these systems. Similarly, the increased range of units adds specificity to text analysis but the unique units can be difficult to understand. To use these tools, teachers need to consider their needs and purposes.

## General Considerations

Because the second-generation formulas have some unique properties, many people are not sure exactly how and when to use them. This section provides some general considerations for using second-generation formulas (Table 3.4). Of course, these considerations should also be used in conjunction with those in Chapter 2 on traditional readability formulas (see Table 2.5).

First, and most importantly, know the units that these second-generation formulas use. Take time to study the scales. Look at the range for a given grade level. Review a list of titles and their text difficulties in Lexiles or DRP. Keep a conversion table taped inside a planning book. Label the spines of teacher editions of textbooks with Lexile or DRP levels. Attach a list of students' reading levels in DRP or Lexiles to a grade book. Being familiar with the meaning of these units is key to using second-generation systems.

Use second-generation formulas when it is possible to obtain both student and text levels in the formula units. A major benefit of these programs is parallel text and reader measures; without pertinent information about both texts and readers, this benefit is lost. Occasionally, teachers may want to convert Lexiles or DRP to grade levels, but, as a practice, it makes absolutely no sense to obtain a student's reading level in grades and then try to convert it to Lexiles or DRP. The precision of text–reader matching using these scales is lost in conversion.

The second-generation formulas make it easy to compare several books. For example, I have used these tools when I have worked on textbook adoption committees. The second-generation formulas helped me to compare two books under consideration for adoption. *The American Nation,* a history text by Davidson, registers at 61 DRP, whereas *The Rise of the American Nation* registers at 67 DRP, a difference of more than two grade levels. David, an intermediate teacher describe in Chapter 7, used Lexiles to compare the novels that he used in his classroom. Second-generation formulas are also very useful to describe student reading levels when grades could be stigmatizing. A number of schools, community colleges, agencies, and prisons use the DRP tests with adult learners. The standard and advanced DRP tests can help identify the basic performance levels of students for placement in graduate equivalency degree or developmental–remedial reading courses. The DRP test is untimed so it is useful for students with learning disabilities.

Last, the second-generation formulas are particularly suited to research endeavors. Their history in the measurement community has strengthened their technical properties.

## SUMMARY

This chapter ends where it began. Everything new was once old. Both Lexiles and DRP are reinventions of classic readability theory. They use

**TABLE 3.4. Guidelines for Using Second-Generation Readability Formulas**

| Guideline | How to apply the guideline |
| --- | --- |
| Know the units. | Because second-generation formulas employ units other than grade levels users must:<br>• Understand the range of the text difficulty units<br>  Lexiles 200–1700<br>  DRP 15–85<br>• Understand the relative meanings of the units<br>  600L—grade 3<br>  48 DRP—grade 3<br>• Keep the scale with grade translations and sample titles handy for quick reference. |
| Use second-generation formulas when you can obtain both the reader and text levels in the formula unit. | The primary benefit of second-generation formulas is the parallel text and reader measures. To take advantage of this benefit:<br>• Use DRP or Lexile-leveled tests to obtain readers' levels.<br>• Use DRP or Lexiles with available reading materials.<br>• As a practice do not use other text and reader measures and then translate reader or text levels into DRP or Lexiles. |
| Use second-generation formulas when you want to compare books. | The properties of the second-generation formulas make them especially helpful in:<br>• Comparing textbooks<br>• Classifying and ordering a large number of tradebooks |
| Use second-generation formulas when there is a reason not to express difficulty in grade levels. | In the following educational settings, Lexiles and DRP are advantageous because they do not rely on grade levels:<br>• With Lexiles and DRP, middle or secondary school remedial programs can avoid the stigma attached to grade levels.<br>• Adult literacy programs also can communicate clients' reading levels without attaching the grade level stigma. |
| Use second-generation formulas for research and test development. | Second-generation formulas were designed by research companies. The following properties make them well-suited to measurement and research:<br>• Interval scale with equal distance between units<br>• Range of units that increases variability in the expression of text difficulty<br>• Strong statistical and technical properties |

the same indices for estimating text difficulty and draw on the same body of research, but they are significantly improved. These tools are fundamentally different because they were created during the technological era. They channel the full power of technology to improve sampling, reliability, and power. I believe that if educators are willing to learn the different metrics of Lexiles and DRP, then these tools are quite helpful, but the unique units can make them cumbersome. The second-generation formulas are the most powerful tools on the market, but their relation to traditional readability formulas assumes all of the same disadvantages.

# CHAPTER 4

# Textual Scaffolds for Beginning Readers
## Qualitative Leveling, Decodability, and Vocabulary Control

Look with favor upon on a bold beginning.
—VIRGIL

Those of us who work with beginning readers know the importance of bold beginnings. If children do not learn to read well in first grade, they are unlikely to improve later (Juel, 1988; Torgeson, 2004; Stanovich, 1985). In fact, no matter what kind of instruction a beginner receives, texts, in part, will shape their success (Menon & Hiebert, 2005; Juel & Roper-Schneider, 1985; Vadasy, Sanders, & Peyton, 2005). Beginning readers test their new knowledge about print in the books that they read. If they cannot use their developing knowledge as they read, then it will be discarded. Understanding the many textual scaffolds that are in place for beginning readers is essential to making a match.

Despite their longevity and reinvention, readability formulas have always been very limited for beginning readers (Fry, 1980; Harris & Jacobson, 1978). Readability formulas are simply not precise enough to address all of the features that affect beginning readers. Yet precision in text–reader matching is most important with beginners because at this stage children do not possess the skills to compensate for difficult passages. Historically, researchers have developed many formats for beginning readers to ameliorate the challenges of the beginning reader. These formats included Webster's Blueback Speller (1828), *McGuffey's Eclectic readers* (McGuffey, 1836), the Elson Basic Readers (Elson & Gray, 1930), the linguistic readers (Bloomfield & Barnhart, 1961), and the literature and Little Books of the 1980s and 1990s (for a full review, see Hoffman, 2002). All of these formats address the primary hurdle of beginning readers: word recognition. To assist readers with word recognition, these formats include a number of special features that go beyond the word frequency and sentence length estimators that are typical of readability formulas. Instead, beginning reading materials may be altered with regard to print size, letter–sound complexity, word repetition, and language patterns. Historically, basal readers limited the introduction of new words, included high-frequency words, or introduced new words with limited letter–sound complexity (i.e., decodable text, phonics readers, or linguistic basals). More recently, qualitative leveling systems, like the Reading Recovery and Fountas–Pinnell systems, have addressed many facets of text difficulty (Fountas & Pinnell, 1999, 2002, 2006; Reading Recovery Council of North America, 2004).

This chapter discusses three textual scaffolds for beginning readers: qualitative leveling systems, decodability, and vocabulary control (Brown, 1999; Mesmer, 1999). The term *textual scaffold* labels the many supports provided in reading textbooks to assist beginners. The term *scaffold* is particularly apropos of beginning reading. In construction work, scaffolds are temporary platforms that support workers who are constructing, improving, or cleaning a structure. Scaffolds are eventually removed. Like the builder's scaffolding, textual scaffolds are also essential and temporary. They support the beginning reader in recognizing words as he or she matures, and they are removed once the reader no longer needs them.

Qualitative leveling systems, decodability, and vocabulary control are derived from distinct theoretical frameworks. Despite their differences, these textual scaffolds coexist in today's classrooms, and teachers must understand how to use them appropriately. Although researchers have heatedly debated the benefits of different beginning reading materials, this book argues that each of these structures *can* and *should* be used in the primary classroom (see, e.g., Allington, 1997; Allington & Woodside-Jiron, 1998; Beck, 1997; Daniels, Zemelman, & Bizar, 1998; Fletcher, Francis, & Foorman, 1997; Kame'enui & Simmons, 1997; Routman, 1997). Skilled teachers understand that there are no panaceas, magic bullets, or perfect beginning reading materials. However, they also understand that there are better text selections that prioritize readers' developmental needs. Certain texts, although imperfect, will better pro-

# WIDELY USED LEVELING SYSTEMS

- **Reading Recovery**
  Grade range:              K–1
  Number of levels:         1–20
  Designation used:         Numbers (1–20)

The Reading Recovery leveling system was brought to the United States from New Zealand (Peterson, 1988). Reading Recovery is a corrective, one-on-one tutoring program for struggling readers in the first grade. Texts used in New Zealand were analyzed and their features distilled and applied to books in the United States. The 20 different levels of the Reading Recovery system make distinctions between books that are necessary for assisting readers who struggle. These same discrepancies may or may not be necessary with normally developing readers. Publishers like Rigby and Wright have published many of the Reading Recovery leveled books.

- **Guided Reading Levels**
  Grade range:              K–6
  Number of levels:         1–26
  Designation used:         Letters (A–Z)
                            Levels A–P for grades K–3
                            Levels J–Z grades 3–6

Fountas and Pinnell, who advanced Reading Recovery in the United States, saw the advantages of the Reading Recovery model for assessing text difficulty. They created a system extending the principles to developmental reading programs for normal readers. Their system did not make the intricate distinctions that the Reading Recovery levels did and extended the system through grade 3 and then through grade 6. The Guided Reading levels use letter labels to distinguish them from the Reading Recovery system.

- **Developmental Reading Assessment (DRA) Levels**
  Grade range:              K–6
  Number of levels:         1–44
  Designation used:         Numbers

Joetta Beaver, author of the Developmental Reading Assessment, applied the tenants of leveling to create another system that extended the Reading Recovery model for a broader range of readers. The unique element of the DRA levels is that they link directly to the assessment. A teacher can use the assessment to obtain the readers' instructional level and then find DRA-leveled books at the appropriate level. The newest version of this test also includes subtests: Phonological Awareness, Metalanguage, Letter/High-Frequency Words, Phonics, Structural Analysis, and Syllabication.

vide what a reader needs at a specific time developmentally. Each text type offers advantages and disadvantages. In earlier eras, teachers were not at liberty to choose between different types of materials, but now qualitatively leveled books, decodable books, and vocabulary-controlled books are often found within a single classroom. (Chapter 6 describes how successful primary-grade teachers select and use various materials in their classrooms.) This chapter describes textual scaffolds for beginning readers and includes tables, equivalency charts, text examples, and a synopsis of the advantages and disadvantages.

## QUALITATIVE LEVELING SYSTEMS

The term *leveling* can have both generic and specific meanings. Generally, the verb form *to level* means to order materials or put them into levels of difficulty. When used in this fashion, the term can refer to any text analysis tools discussed in this book because each tool levels books. Specifically, the term can refer to an approach to text analysis with a particular history, one that focuses on a set qualitative text features. In this chapter, the term *qualitative leveling* refers to the specific approach to text analysis and not to the general process of ordering materials.

In a 2006 survey, more than 70% of K–3 teachers reported using leveled text three or more times per week (Mesmer, 2006). Currently, qualitative leveling systems are very popular. These systems include the Reading Recovery levels, the Fountas–Pinnell Guided Reading levels, and the Development Reading Assessment levels in addition to many lesser known, but similar, systems (Brooks, 1996; Fountas & Pinnell, 1999, 2002, 2006; Hart-Hewins & Wells, 1999; Miller, 2000; Peterson, 2001; Syymusiak & Sibberson, 2001; Weaver, 2000). (See the boxes on pages 65 and 68–69 for examples of widely used systems and teacher resources.) In addition, the past 10 years have witnessed the publication of a number of teacher resource books detailing qualitative leveling systems. This section gives an overview of qualitative leveling. It will not fully educate the reader about the intricacies of each of the 15+ levels in the most popular systems. It will not teach the reader how to level books. Other authors have done this well. What this section *will* do is help the reader to understand leveling within the context of readability as a whole and to use it appropriately.

Authors use the term *text gradient* to describe qualitative leveling systems (Fountas & Pinnell, 1999). A text gradient consists of books that gradually increase in difficulty. It is like a hill, with the difficulty gradually increasing as the hill slopes upward. The qualitative leveling system marks the difficulty of books. The purpose of qualitative leveling systems is to provide manageable increments. Qualitative leveling systems were originally created for beginning reading, but some have been extended into the intermediate grades (Fountas & Pinnell, 1999, 2002, 2006; Peterson, 1988, 2001).

To understand qualitative leveling is to understand its path to the United States. In a 1988 unpublished dissertation, Peterson described a process that New Zealand teachers used to classify books (Peterson, 1988; School Publications Branch, 1985). Peterson later published a book describing this process (Peterson, 2001). This New Zealand system was adopted by Reading Recovery and then extended for classroom use by Fountas and Pinnell (1999, 2002).

Qualitative leveling systems order books by assigning holistic difficulty labels. Holistic means that the label describes the entire book by integrating information about many text features. The labels are descriptive and qualitative rather than quantitative. The labels are *not* based on counting features like the number of words in a sentence or the number of syllables in a word. Instead, qualitative leveling systems address many different text features and then rely on a composite difficulty label, usually a letter, to represent the difficulty of a book. People assign levels to individual books and then test the books with readers. This human component distinguishes qualitative leveling systems from other systems that rely on computer analyses or formulas. Qualitative leveling systems represent an ordinal scale rather than an interval scale. The levels order books by difficulty but the distance between levels is not equal interval. A Level C book and a Level D book may not be equally different as a Level D book and a level E book.

Depending on the system, between 15 and 26 difficulty labels, or levels, are used. The term *book bands,* used in the United Kingdom, further elucidates the concept. Books within the same band or level possess similar levels of difficulty and are theoretically exchangeable. For instance, two Level C books should be similarly difficult. Each book level addresses a number of features, and these features change as the levels increase so that the system addresses the needs of readers at different stages of development. Qualitative leveling systems address three major features: language, content, and format.

Theoretically, qualitative leveling systems seem to align with interactive models of reading (Rumelhart, 1994). The interactive model posits that readers draw on different sources of information as they recognize words, including (1) syntax (grammatical expectations); (2) semantics (meaning–vocabulary); (3) orthography (letters–sounds and spelling); and (4) lexicon (sight word stores possessed by the reader). As readers recognize words, they cross-check the printed word with the letters–sounds that they see, the kinds of words that would work grammatically in a sentence, word meanings, and sight knowledge of words

## TEACHER RESOURCES FOR USING LEVELED TEXT

- **Brooks, E. J. (1996).** *Just-right books for beginning readers: Leveled booklists and strategies*. **New York: Scholastic.**
- **Fountas, I., & Pinnell, G. S. (1996).** *Guided reading: Good first teaching for all children.* **Portsmouth, NH: Heinemann.**
- **Fountas, I., & Pinnell, G. S. (1999).** *Matching books to readers: Using leveled books in guided reading, K–3.* **Portsmouth, NH: Heinemann.**
- **Fountas, I., & Pinnell, G. S. (2002).** *Leveled books for readers: Grades 3– 6.* **Portsmouth, NH: Heinemann.**
- **Fountas, I., & Pinnell, G. S. (2006).** *The Fountas and Pinnell leveled book list, K–8 2006–2008 edition.* **Portsmouth, NH: Heinemann.**

  Fountas and Pinnell's inventive books have had significant impact on classrooms around the country. They can be credited with bringing leveling to the regular classroom by creating Guided Reading levels, a system rooted in the principles of the Reading Recovery levels. The first of this collection, the *Guided Reading* book, focuses mostly on the Guided Reading teaching method but includes one chapter about text leveling and includes lists of books. However, the three following this text directly address text leveling for K–3 readers and for third through eighth graders. About two thirds of each of these volumes are composed of extensive lists of more than 5,000 leveled books. Books are listed alphabetically by title and by level. Book titles, authors, levels, and publishers are listed. The Fountas–Pinnell tomes are handy book list references.

- **Hart-Hewins, L., & Wells, J. (1999).** *Better books! Better readers: How to choose, use, and level books for children in primary grades.* **Portland, ME: Stenhouse.**

  The focus of this comprehensive book is on practical teaching ideas and organizational strategies for the elementary teacher who wants to build a literacy program based on trade titles. The book illustrates stages of development, processes for choosing books, and processes for leveling books. Although this book includes an extensive bibliography of tradebooks at the end, the focus is not specifically on leveling.

- **Miller, A. (2000).** *Book steps: Leveled trade books for guided reading, independent reading, and authentic assessment.* **Winnipeg, Manitoba, Canada: Portage & Main Press.**

  In this spiral-bound text for pre-K to third grade, Miller describes the development of literacy. With special attention to stages of development, Miller then identifies appropriate leveled books. The second part of the book is a list of more than 600 trade titles that have been assigned one of 15 levels using her system. The advantage of this text is the annotations, which are not found in other resources, and the identification of pre-K books.

*(continued)*

- **Reading Recovery Council of North America. (2004). *Reading Recovery book list 2004*. Columbus, OH: Author.**

  This resource is an annual list published by the Reading Recovery Council of North America. It includes titles and Reading Recovery levels for more than 2,500 books listed by title, publisher, and level. The books in the list are recommended for use in Reading Recovery but could also be used with beginning readers in kindergarten through grade 2. The beauty of this list is that the titles have been used extensively by teachers in actual instructional settings.

- **Peterson, B. (2001). *Literary pathways: Selecting books to support new readers*. Portsmouth, NH: Heinemann.**

  In 1988 Barbara Peterson analyzed some of the first collections of Reading Recovery books used in this country. This compact book provides a careful explanation of how leveling works from someone who has studied it closely. It includes detailed discussions of many leveled books and thoroughly elucidates the subtleties of leveling for beginning readers. It also includes annotated bibliographies of books arranged around different themes. This book is for the reader who wants to understand the Reading Recovery leveling system in depth.

- **Syymusiak, K., & Sibberson, F. (2001). *Beyond leveled books: Supporting transitional grades 2–5*. Portsmouth, ME: Stenhouse.**

  This interesting book written by two teachers challenges the notion of leveling for readers in the intermediate grades. It argues that other perspectives on text difficulty can be and should be used for these readers. The text is more than a "how-to" for matching readers and books, with practical teaching and organizational strategies.

- **Weaver, B. M. (2000). *Leveling books K–6: Matching readers to text*. Newark, DE: International Reading Association.**

  Weaver has assembled a simple book linking development, assessment, and books together. In this work she describes literacy development using the Weaver Reading/Writing Stages, compares various leveling systems, and shows how to link books with stages of development. Glossary and examples of books included.

(Clay, 1985). Take, for instance, the word *store* in the following sentence: "We shop in the (store)." To identify *store*, a reader would integrate information about the letters–sounds, part of speech, and meaning of the word. Syntactically, the reader would expect a noun in this place in the sentence. Semantically the target word must relate to shopping and visually the beginning of the word must begin with /s/. If the word *store* was in the reader's sight word collection, then it would be automatically accessed. Theoretically, qualitative leveling systems appear to support teaching approaches that emphasize successful coordination of multiple sources of information.

## Language: Sentence Complexity, Organization, Style, and Predictability

One element of text difficulty considered within the qualitative leveling systems is language. The language of books spans many difficulty levels. The complexity of the sentences, style of the language, text organization, and predictability will influence how a reader approaches a text. Simpler levels contain simple sentences with structures that are familiar to children. Often these levels include sentences with a clear subject and predicate nucleus or those that follow a command structure that children use in their own speech. The book *Look at Me* contains very simple syntax: "I like to run fast. Look at me. I like to jump high. Look at me. I like to read every day." More difficult levels contain compound or complex sentences with dependent phrases and embedded clauses. The style of language used may also influence readers. The text in the opening pages of the book *Get Well, Good Knight* (Thomas, 2002) reads, "Once there were three little dragons. They lived in a dark cave. The cave was in a dense forest. The forest was in a faraway kingdom. The poor little dragons were not feeling well" (p. 5). The phrases *once upon a time, dense forest, faraway kingdom, deep dark cave,* all belong to a literary genre: the fairytale. Most children do not use words like *kingdom* and *faraway* in their own language. This language is especially unfamiliar to children who have had few experiences with books. Children will find language that emulates their oral structures easier than literary or technical language.

In the simpler texts, each page will contain brief, single sentences. As texts become more difficult, pages become denser with many sentences that build into paragraphs. The paragraphs then link into sections, which are divided into chapters. In books with chapters and paragraphs, readers must follow and remember multiple events. They must also know what to expect as they read books with denser text.

Finally, at the easiest levels, readers can count on predictability. Predictable language is marked by rhyming and repetitive sentence patterns. Many young children have enjoyed the predictable language in *Brown Bear, Brown Bear, What Do You See?* (Martin, 1995): "Brown bear, brown bear, what do you see? I see a red bird looking at me. Red bird, red bird, what do you see? I see a yellow duck looking at me. " *Brown Bear* illustrates predictable supports. Sentences and phrases repeat in memorable configurations. As texts become more difficult, the predictable language and rhyming are abandoned.

## Content: Familiarity, Genre, and Vocabulary

One of the major differences between qualitative leveling systems and other text difficulty tools, like readability formulas, is that leveling addresses content. The content of a text may influence its difficulty because readers' prior knowledge will interact with this content. Settings, themes, and content that are familiar to readers are simpler than those that are unfamiliar. I cannot read even the simplest mechanical engineering book but can digest reading research pieces that are more complex. For children, the simplest books revolve around universal activities that take place in the home and school (e.g., mealtime, playing, going to sleep, cooking, getting up in the morning). In contrast, more complex books contain content that is removed from the experiences of the reader. Easier texts have content that is concrete and observable as opposed to abstract. For example, many young children would find discussions about planetary movement abstract and challenging to grasp.

A book's genre is the category in which it is placed. Literary genres include contemporary narratives, fairytales, folklore, poetry, historical fiction, fantasy, science fiction, and informational texts on history, science, or social studies. Simple narratives are stories with a single setting, a clear resolution, and a clear problem. More complex narratives may be episodic and contain multiple settings. For example, in *Frog and Toad Are Friends* (Lobel, 1979), Frog and Toad move from place to place as they have their adventures. The most complex narratives use subplots, flashback, or different points of view. Generally, books that are high fantasy, historical fiction, or scientific are more difficult to young children. Information texts include multiple headings, subheadings, labeled diagrams, charts, tables, sidebars, glossaries, and indexes. Figure 4.1 presents *Parts of a Plant* illustrating the interplay among texts, photographs, captions, and sidebars.

Finally, the level of the vocabulary will impact difficulty. Vocabulary refers to the words used in text and their meanings. The easiest books limit vocabulary to simple words that are used often in spoken language. In easy books, the range of vocabulary will be narrower. More difficult books will use a wider variety of words that communicate subtle distinctions in meaning. In a simple book, the word *angry* may be used, but in a more complex book the words *livid, annoyed, agitated,* or *explosive* might express shades of meaning. Difficult books also contain language that is more technical. Technical words that are particular to a field can be more difficult. For example, *Slinky, Scaly Snakes!* (Royston, 1998) contains the word "molting," introducing the reader to a domain-specific word. In high fantasy invented vocabulary may appear. The *Harry Potter* series includes the game of *Quidditch* and the label *Muggles.*

**Parts of a Plant**

Just like people, plants have different parts that serve different purposes.

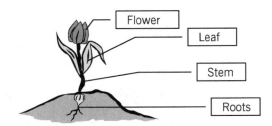

Each plant has **roots, stems, leaves,** and **flowers.**
*A picture of the plant and its parts.*

**Roots**

Roots are very important to the plant. The roots anchor the plant to the ground so that it does not get pulled up or blown away. The roots also help the plant collect water and food. Roots store food for the plant to use later.

**Roots we eat**

Many people do not know it but we eat the roots of certain plants. Beets, sweet potatoes, and celery are examples of root vegetables. The roots of plants are usually filling and starchy.

**FIGURE 4.1.** An example of a nonfiction text: *Parts of a Plant.*

## Text Format: Length, Print, Layout, and Illustrations

New readers will not be able to negotiate the text layout in the same way as more mature readers. Unlike other systems, qualitative leveling systems address formatting. Formatting refers to a book's appearance and organization. Book length (in words and pages), print style and size, layout, and illustrations can make a big difference. Books with fewer words are considered easier (Hatcher, 2000).

Print style, size, and spacing can all influence text difficulty. Font styles can be large and very clear (e.g., Helvetica) or they can be tighter and smaller like the font in which this book is set. In addition, print size can be a standard 10 or 12 points or a larger and easier-to-read 18 or 20 points. Furthermore, spaces between words can be l a r g e r, making words more distinct, or they can be smaller, creating a denser text space.

How publishers organize a book is also very important. I remember asking first graders to read a version of *Cinderella* (Frost & Jackman, 2000, see Figure 4.2). The comic book-style presentation with the speech bubbles was interesting but challenging because every page placed text in a different place and the order for reading the text bubbles did not follow the typical left-to-right, top-to-bottom orientation of print.

In the easiest books, readers can find the text in the very same location on every page. In *I Get Dressed* (Cutting, 1988) (Figure 4.3), the text is in the middle of the page right below the illustration. A young reader would know exactly where to look on each page to begin reading. The nonfiction example, *Parts of a Plant*, has print in a caption under

**FIGURE 4.2.** *Cinderella.* Copyright 2000 by Sundance Publishing. Reprinted by permission.

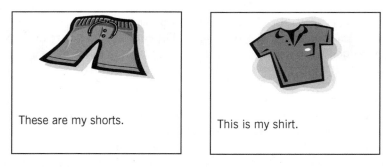

**FIGURE 4.3.** *I Get Dressed.*

the picture, in a labeled drawing, and in the body of the text. Sometimes even an experienced reader might not know exactly where to start. As readers become more advanced, they should be able to handle a layout with print in several different and inconsistent locations.

The number of illustrations and connection between print and picture also influences complexity. Books with few illustrations are more demanding than books in which illustrations subsume two thirds or more of the page space. Pictures at the earliest stages will help children recognize words. In the easiest books, for instance, pictures mirror the print. The example *I Get Dressed* contains highly supportive illustrations because the words name the items of clothing that the character is using in each picture. In more advanced books, pictures may be absent all together or may only enhance the printed story.

Figure 4.4 summarizes the text features addressed in qualitative leveling systems. This basic figure does not list all of the subtleties of qualitative leveling systems. It does, however, serve as a handy tool for getting the gist of leveling. For illustrative purposes, Table 4.1 translates the Fountas–Pinnell levels into grade levels and Table 4.2 qualitatively describes the Fountas–Pinnell levels.

**Easiest Books**                              **More Difficult Books**

| Text Feature | Moving from | To |
|---|---|---|
| **Content** | | |
| • **Familiarity** | Material that is within the readers' experiences | Material that is abstract or removed from the readers' experiences |
| • **Genre** | Simple narratives and expository books Straightforward plots, single themes | Historical fiction, complex expository books, memoir, high fantasy Episodic plots, complex characters, multiple themes |
| • **Vocabulary** | A narrow range of words that are common to oral language | A broad range of words that are limited to specific fields or written contexts |
| **Language** | | |
| • **Sentence complexity** | Simple subject–predicate formats | Compound or complex structures with embedded clauses and phrases |
| • **Organization** | Single sentences on a page | Paragraphs, headed sections, chapters |
| • **Style** | Language reflecting oral structures | Language that is literary or technical |
| • **Predictability** | Patterned language, repeated sentences, rhyming | Sentences without repeated formats or rhyming |
| **Format** | | |
| • **Length** | Short books with 50 words or less | Longer books with more than 250 words |
| • **Print** | Large, clear fonts with space between letters and words | Smaller, tighter fonts with less space between letters and words |
| • **Layout** | Print is in the same location on a page | Print is in different locations on each page Sidebars, headings, labels |
| • **Illustrations** | Pictures on every page, pictures directly represent words | Few infrequent pictures that only enhance text |

**FIGURE 4.4.** A summary of the text features addressed in qualitative leveling systems.

**TABLE 4.1. Translation of Fountas–Pinnell Levels**

|  | Grade | Fountas–Pinnell level[a] | Basal level | Reading Recovery |
|---|---|---|---|---|
| Emergent | Kindergarten Grade 1 | A | Readiness | 1 |
| Early | Kindergarten Grade 1 | B |  | 2 |
|  | Kindergarten Grade 1 | C | PP1 | 3 and 4 |
|  | Grade 1 | D | PP2 | 5 and 6 |
|  | Grade 1 | E | PP3 | 7 and 8 |
|  | Grade 1 | F | Primer | 9 and 10 |
|  | Grade 1 | G |  | 11 and 12 |
| Transitional | Grade 1 | H | Grade 1 | 13 and 14 |
|  | Grade 1 Grade 2 | I |  | 15, 16, 17 |
|  | Grade 2 | J | Grade 2 | 18, 19, 20 |
|  | Grade 2 | K |  |  |
|  | Grade 2 | L |  |  |
|  | Grade 2 Grade 3 | M |  |  |
| Self-extending | Grade 3 | N | Grade 3 |  |
|  | Grade 3 | O |  |  |
|  | Grade 3 Grade 4 | P |  |  |
|  | Grade 4 | Q | Grade 4 |  |
|  | Grade 4 | R |  |  |
| Advanced | Grade 4 | S |  |  |

*Note.* All levels and equivalencies are approximations and are subject to revision. Reprinted by permission from *Matching Books to Readers* by Irene C. Fountas and Gay Su Pinnell. Copyright 1999 by Irene C. Fountas and Gay Su Pinnell. Published by Heinemann, a division of Reed Elsevier, Inc., Portsmouth, NH. All rights reserved.
[a]Fountas and Pinnell (1996).

## Research on Qualitative Leveling Systems

Researchers have examined leveled texts both formally and informally. The most recent and thorough analysis of qualitative leveling systems was conducted by Cunningham et al. (2005). Researchers analyzed a set of 80 texts leveled using the Reading Recovery system and found that the system was stronger in some respects than others. They found that Reading Recovery levels tended to differ at the whole text level. For instance, the best predictor of a Reading Recovery level was the number of unique words in a book, accounting for some 47% of variance. Essentially, as levels increased, the primary text feature that changed was the number of different words. More difficult books have higher total word

**TABLE 4.2. Qualitative Descriptions of the Kindergarten and First-Grade Levels of the Fountas–Pinnell Levels**

| Level | Description of texts |
|---|---|
| Levels A and B | Books have a simple story line, and a direct correspondence between pictures and text. Children can relate to the topic. Language includes naturally occurring structures. Print appears at the same place on each page and is regular, clear, and easy to see. Print is clearly separated from pictures. There are clear separations between words so children can point and read. Several frequent words are repeated often. Most books have one to four lines of text per page. Many "caption books" (e.g., labeled pictures) are included in Level A. Level B may have more lines and a slightly broader range of vocabulary. |
| Level C | Books have simple story lines and reflect familiar topics, but tend to be longer (more words, somewhat longer sentences) than Level B books, even though there may be only two to five lines of text per page. Familiar oral language structures may be repeated, and phrasing may be supported by placement on the page. The story is carried by the text, however, and children must attend closely to print at some points because of variation in patterns. Even so, there is still a direct correspondence between pictures and text. |
| Level D | Stories are a bit more complex and longer than previous levels, but still reflective of children's experiences. More attention to the print is required, even though illustrations continue to support the reading. Most texts at this level have clear print and obvious spacing. Most frequently, there are two to six lines of print per page. There is a full range of punctuation. Words that were encountered in previous texts may be used many times. Vocabulary may contain inflectional endings. |
| Level E | Stories are slightly more complex and longer; some concepts may be more subtle and require interpretation. Even when patterns repeat, the patterns vary. There may be three to eight lines of text per page, but text placement varies. Although illustrations support the stories, the illustrations contain several ideas. Words are longer, may have inflectional endings, and may require analysis. A full variety of punctuation is evident. |
| Level F | Texts are slightly longer than the previous level, and the print is somewhat smaller. There are usually three to eight lines of text per page. Meaning is carried more by the text than the pictures. The syntax is more like written than oral language, but the pattern is mixed. The variety of frequent words expands. There are many opportunities for word analysis. Stories are characterized by more episodes, which follow chronologically. Dialogue has greater variety. Punctuation supports phrasing and meaning. |
| Levels G and H | Books contain more challenging ideas and vocabulary, with longer sentences. Content may not be within children's experiences. There are typically four to eight lines of text per page. As at Level F, literary language is integrated with more natural language patterns. Stories have more events. Occasionally, episodes repeat. Level H differs from Level G in that the language and vocabulary become more complex and there is less episodic repetition. |
| Level I | A variety of types of texts may be represented. They are longer, with more sentences per page. Story structure is more complex, with more elaborate episodes and varied themes. Illustrations provide less support, although they extend the texts. Specialized and more unusual vocabulary are included. |

*Note.* From Hoffman, Roser, Salas, Patterson, and Pennington (2001). Copyright 2001 by the National Reading Conference. Reprinted by permission.

counts. This suggests that the approach to difficulty centers on the number of words that a reader must remember within a book. In addition, one sentence-level variable distinguished books of different difficulties. Sentence patterns, as measured by T units, did coincide with the oral language patterns of first graders (Cunningham et al., 2005). Thus, the syntactic structures in the books did appear to support readers.

Cunningham et al. (2005) also found that words were not controlled by word frequency or decodability. Indeed, this type of control was never an intention in leveled texts. Peterson (1988) wrote, "[Children are] able to read and learn from challenging, difficult texts. It is unnecessary to provide specialized texts with severely controlled vocabulary for beginning readers." Analysis of levels showed that words in leveled texts did not consistently increase in letter–sound complexity at the phonogram level (e.g., *-ag, -et, -eat, -ight*), indicating that they were probably not highly supportive of onset–rime decoding (Cunningham et al., 2005). Teachers have also noticed this. Brabham and Villaume (2002) wrote, "Some students experience [frustration] when they try to apply what they have learned about letter–sound relationships to the large number of phonetically irregular words" (p. 440). I experienced the same frustration myself. I had first graders reading a Level F book, *Itchy, Itchy Chicken Pox* (Maccorone, 1992). The text reads:

> A spot, a spot, another spot. Uh-oh chicken pox! Under my shirt. Under my socks. Itchy, itchy chicken pox. Don't rub. Don't scratch. Oh no! another batch. On my tummy, between my toes, down my back, on my nose. Lotion on, itching's gone just for now. (Maccarone, 1992, pp. 2–6)

Words liked *itchy, batch,* and *lotion* were quite tricky.

Hatcher (2000) analyzed about 200 Reading Recovery books and found that the key distinction between levels was at the book level. In Hatcher's study, the following five variables predicted about 83% of the variance in Reading Recovery levels: (1) sentence length; (2) word length; (3) syntactic features; (4) number of pages; and (5) number of words. This means that the assigned Reading Recovery levels were highly related to these five features of text. Interestingly, many of these same features, like word and sentence length, are traditional readability indices.

Books that have been qualitatively leveled do tend to include many high-content words, words that relate to the theme and pictures in the book (Hiebert, 1998). Words like *elephant, spaceship,* and *dinosaur* have rich meanings and are critical to story comprehension but difficult to fully decode (Hiebert, 1998). Hoffman, Roser, Salas, Patterson, and

Pennington (2001) found that Fountas–Pinnell levels did predict student accuracy and fluency. Students read the more difficult levels with less accuracy and fluency than the easier levels.

In sum, current evidence suggests that qualitative leveling systems are valid ways to order books if the basis of difficulty is text length, syntactic difficulty, and student accuracy–fluency. In this regard, a Level A book will be easier than a Level B book, which will be easier than a Level C book. However, word-level distinctions, like word frequency and decodability, do not distinguish levels. Books at the lower levels are just as likely to include few high-frequency words and complex letters–sounds as books at the higher levels.

## Advantages and Disadvantages of Qualitative Leveling Systems

As Marie Clay explained, "All [text] gradients are inevitably fallible" (1991, p. 201). Like any other system, teachers will find that qualitative leveling systems have both advantages and disadvantages. The first advantage of the leveling systems is that they have broadened notions of text difficulty in beginning reading. Qualitative leveling systems have brought to the forefront considerations of formatting, illustrations, content, and language that previous materials ignored.

Second, the qualitative leveling systems added divisions to the pre-primer, primer, and first-grade categories that traditionally have defined difficulty levels in beginning reading materials. By parsing the very simplest materials into even more discrete categories, qualitative leveling systems have offered beginning readers greater levels of support. The third advantage of the qualitative leveling systems is that they build on the judgment of experienced teachers working with young readers. Most of the leveled books in the Fountas–Pinnell collection and all of the Reading Recovery titles are field tested. This element increases the system's credibility.

No one system can work for all children all of the time, and qualitative leveling systems are no different. Qualitative leveling systems do not offer support at the word level. Books are not designed to introduce children to increasingly complex letter–sound information or sets of high-frequency words (Cunningham et al., 2005). Instead, the number of words and language support reading. Teachers working with beginning readers have identified this drawback (Brabham & Villaume, 2002). In a research study, I asked first graders to read the Level F book *Going Shopping* (Prince, 1999). The text reads, "I went shopping with my mom. We went to the hardware store. I didn't want to. We went to the ice cream store. I wanted to." The word *hardware* is a two-syllable word with two difficult vowel patterns: /ar/ and /are/. Although the pictures and the context should assist the reader in coming up with the word "hardware," I found that many readers said the word "hammer" instead of "hardware" even when rereading the book.

A second disadvantage of leveling systems is that they may have some reliability issues (Dreyfuss, 2002; Fry, 2002; Gunning, 2003; Hiebert, 2002). In some instances, levels are difficult for people to apply consistently with the same results. Assigning levels requires a person to attend to a number of different features at the same time and then assign a level. Dreyfus (2002) found that at the higher levels (J and above) actual difficulties could vary. When books at these levels were evaluated using Degrees of Reading Power (DRP), the obtained difficulties in levels ranged as much as 2 years. (Dreyfus, however, is a vice president for research at Touchstone Applied Science and Associates, Inc., [now Questar Assessment] owner of DRP.) Some measures of interrater reliability would significantly improve the qualitative leveling systems. Interrater reliability indicates how frequently different people leveling the same materials would assign the same level. In addition, the feature categories—language, content, and format—are not weighted or balanced in the leveling process, so there is no way to ensure that each set of features are equally addressed in the process (Hiebert & Mesmer, 2006). One book might be considered a Level A primarily because of formatting, whereas another might receive the Level A designation because of language or content. Essentially, leveling has enhanced and broadened text difficulty, but word level difficulty and reliability are disadvantages.

## DECODABILITY

In 2003, the International Reading Association conducted a survey of influential reading professionals. More than 50% of respondents believed that decodable text was a trend in literacy instruction, but the same percentage believed that it should not be (Cassidy & Cassidy, 2003). Between about 1987 and 1997, decodable text was virtually absent from the educational market but with the 2000 basals, decodable text resurfaced (Foorman, Francis, Davidson, Harm, & Griffin, 2005; Hiebert & Mesmer, 2006; Hoffman, Sailors, & Patterson, 2003; Stein, Johnson, & Gutlohn, 1999). In fact, decodable texts or phonics readers are now available through all the major educational publishing houses and are packaged with all of the first-grade basals. The reemergence of decodable texts has been quite controversial. Some are fearful that recent changes will fill classrooms with dull materials (Allington, 1997; Routman, 1997). Others argue that decodable text has a place in beginning reading instruction (Beck, 1997; Fletcher et al., 1997; Hoffman et al., 2001; Kame'enui & Simmons, 1997; Stein et al., 1999). Interestingly, primary teachers do not report extreme views. In a 2006 survey, K–3 teachers reported using decodable text moderately and for very specific purposes, like teaching decoding and working with struggling readers (Mesmer, 2006).

Perhaps for good reasons controversy has surrounded decodable text, but this section focuses on defining this class of textual scaffolding, detailing current research, and describing the advantages and disadvantages. This will allow readers to decide for themselves how they might use decodable text in their own classrooms. Chapter 6 describes a primary teacher using decodable texts.

## The Elements of Decodable Text:
## Regularity and Instructional Consistency

As a textual scaffold, decodability supports readers in sounding out words. Theoretically, proponents of decodable texts adhere to reading models that emphasize letter–sound knowledge as the prioritized strategy to identify words. In Ehri's research-supported theory of word recognition, readers increasingly use letter–sound knowledge to recognize words (Ehri, 2005; Ehri & McCormick, 1998). Readers begin at a prealphabetic phase in which they do not use letters–sounds to identify words but instead rely on paired associations, such as double letters, logos (e.g., McDonald's), length, or any other idiosyncratic feature. At a partial alphabetic phase, readers use initial sounds and context clues to recognize words. At the full alphabetic phase, they fully decode words, blending the consonants and vowels; at the consolidated alphabetic phase, they consolidate multiletter units (e.g., *sh*, *ee*, *oi*, *ing*) to speedily recognized multisyllable words. Importantly, Ehri's amalgamation theory suggests that repeatedly applying letter–sound knowledge to decode words sears words permanently into sight word vocabulary. Decodable texts enable readers to focus on letter–sound knowledge. Today's decodable texts contain two features: (1) regular relationships between letters and sounds; and (2) a correspondence between the letters–sounds appearing in text and those that the reader has been taught (Mesmer, 2001a, 2001b). This section briefly describes how these two text elements work in decodable text.

The word *regular* is described as "customary, usual, normal, orderly, even, in conformity, and constant." When researchers say that decodable texts present *regular* letters–sounds, they mean that, within words, the letters consistently map onto specific sounds (Cunningham et al., 2005; Juel & Roper-Schneider, 1985). Letters, then, represent their usual or customary sounds, and representations that do not conform to focal letter–sound patterns are not presented within a text. For example, the book *Tim's Lost Fan* (Dobeck, 2002) is a decodable text that emphasizes the short /a/ and /i/ sounds. The book reads, "Tim's fan is lost. Is his fan at the top? Is Tim's fan on the mat? Is his fan in the pit? Tim's fan is not lost" (pp. 2–5). The book does not present words with the letter a representing anything other than the short sound (e.g., b*a*ker, c*a*r, s*a*y, *a*bout). The consistency in letters–sounds allows readers to practice reading short /a/ words in context without confusion or frustration. As a textual scaffold, regularity relates to readers and what they know about letters–sounds. The word *car*, for instance, is not irregular if the focal pattern of a book is *r*-controlled vowel sounds and the reader is learning this pattern.

In 1961, Bloomfield and Barnhart formally proposed that words in texts should be ordered by regular letters–sounds. Their program, *Let's Read: A Linguistic Approach* presented the beginning reader with a systematically ordered set of letter–sound elements that were clustered and repeated within stories. This ordered set of regular elements was intended to actually *do* the phonics teaching. Bloomfield and Barnhart (1961) wrote, "[The child] does not need phonics instruction because like words are arranged together so that the pattern of the words is obvious" (p. 10). In the original work, therefore, decodable text referred only to clustering like patterns together in text.

The research literature defines regularity as a sublexical characteristic, meaning that regularity refers to word parts (Cunningham et al., 2005; Hoffman et al., 2001; Menon & Hiebert, 1999). Researchers have found that highly decodable texts repeat rhymes or phonograms (e.g., -at, -ack, -ash) within a text (Hiebert, 1998; Juel & Roper-Schneider, 1985). Thus, a decodable text might contain the words *bash*, *cash*, and *dash* to allow the reader to acquire the subunit, *ash*. Regularity often focuses on vowel patterns because consistency at this level helps beginning readers to negotiate the 19 vowel phonemes in English (Ehri & McCormick, 1998). Most decodable texts list the focal phonics elements present to make using the books easier. Figure 4.5 provides an example of such a listing with focal letter–sound patterns and high-frequency words.

There appears to be a widely accepted scope and sequence for presenting letters–sounds to the reader, one that remains consistent across many different titles and books. Table 4.3 presents this sequence (Menon & Hiebert, 1999). In most decodable books, short vowels within simple consonant-vowel-consonant words are the easiest to decode (e.g., *get*, *can*, *fun*). Then books add consonant blends and digraphs to the short vowel patterns (e.g., *ship*, *chin*, *thin*). In more difficult decodable books, long-vowel, *r*-controlled, and diphthong patterns are presented and, lastly, multisyllable words. Note that this sequence progresses from simple one-to-one letter–sound correspondences to more complex two-to-one or three-to-one correspondences. Hence, regularity in decodable text

---

**A Trap!**

**Grade 1**

**In this book:**

**Decoding practice for the following letter–sound patterns:**

| Short *a, e, o, u, i* | *tr* (trap, trip, trim) |
| *fl* (flops) | *gr* (grab) |
| *br* (brag) | *pr* (prod) |

**High-frequency words:**

**Decodable:**

| can | it |
| is | get |
| at | off |
| ran | |

**Nondecodable:**

| see | do |
| you | of |
| to | |

---

**FIGURE 4.5.** Listing of phonics elements in a decodable book.

focuses mostly on rhymes, keeping vowel graphemes consistent, and following a customary scope and sequence.

With calls for explicit, systematic phonics instruction, today's decodable texts remind teachers to pay attention to a second feature: instructional consistency. Instructional consistency is the coordination between the words in text and the phonics instruction (Foorman et al., 2004; Hoffman et al., 2003; Mesmer, 2001a; Stein et al., 1999). Generally, the logic is that if words are to be decodable, then children must be taught the requisite knowledge to decode them. In research studies, instructional consistency is the percentage of words matching prescribed phonics lessons. If, for example, the child has received instruction in the sounds /i/ and /o/ and then encounters a number of words with these sounds (e.g., *his, pot, got, fit*), the instructional consistency would be high. If a low percentage of words in text match phonics lessons, then the instructional consistency would be low.

Percentages of instructional consistency vary (Barr & Dreeben, 1983; Beck & Block, 1978; Foorman et al., 2004; Stein, 1993; Stein et al., 1999). In one review of research, highly decodable text had an average 64% of words matching lessons (Mesmer, 2001b). A 2004 analysis of basals pub-

**TABLE 4.3. A Sequence for the Letter–Sound Complexity of Words**

| Level | Pattern | Excludes | Examples |
|---|---|---|---|
| 1 | A, I<br>C-V | | A, I<br>me, we, be, he, my, by, so, go, no |
| 2 | C-V-C<br>V-C | No words ending in r or l | man, cat, hot<br>am, an, as, at, ax<br>if, in, is, it<br>on, ox<br>up, us |
| 3 | C-C-V<br>V-C-C-(C)<br>C-C-(C)-V-C<br>C-V-C-C-(C)<br>C-C-(C)-V-C-C-(C) | Words ending in r or l r-C or l-C (e.g., fort, mild) or V-gh (sigh, eight) | she, the, who, why, cry, dry<br>ash, itch<br>that, chat, brat, scrap<br>back, mash, catch<br>crash, track, scratch |
| 4 | (C)-(C)-(C)-V-C-e | | bake, ride, mile, plate, ate |
| 5 | C-(C)-V-V-(C)-(C)<br>V-V-C-(C) | No words ending in -gh (e.g., laugh, though) | beat, tree, say, paid<br>eat, each |
| 6 | C-(C)-V-r<br>(C)-(C)-V-r-C<br>(C)-(C)-V-ll<br>C-(C)-V-l-C<br>C-(C)-V-V-l-C | | car, scar, fir<br>farm, start, art, arm<br>all, ball, shall, tell, will<br>told, child<br>could, should, field, build |
| 7 | Dipthongs | | boy, oil, draw, cloud |
| 8 | Multisyllabic words | | dinosaur, petulant |

Note. From Menon and Hiebert (1999). Copyright 1999 by Shailaja Menon and Elfrieda Hiebert. Reprinted by permission.

lished after 2000 showed that instructional consistency ranged from about 16 to 70%, with an average of about 43% (Foorman et al., 2004). Instructional consistency has formed the cornerstone of decodability definitions in state policy documents (California Department of Education, 1996; Texas Education Agency, 1997). Interestingly, these policies stipulate instructional consistencies of 75 to 80%, a percentage few existing programs meet (California Department of Education, 1999). Furthermore, all of these percentages are based on the assumption that the phonics lessons in teacher's editions are all taught and in the manner and sequence described in the guide. In reality, teachers frequently deviate from teacher's editions. The notion of instructional consistency is a good one because readers need to see that word recognition strategies work within the context of connected reading. However, an optimal percentage of instructional consistency does not exist.

## Evaluating Decodable Text

As mentioned earlier, teachers can easily find decodable text or phonics readers. However, not all decodable materials are high quality. In fact, a major problem with decodable text is that no one has articulated the difference between high-quality and low-quality materials. Many low-quality examples are used to describe this class of materials. In 2003, Jenkins, Vadasy, Peyton, and Sanders wrote an article in *The Reading Teacher* entitled "Decodable Text: Where to Find It." They identified the *Bob Books for Young Readers (Sets 1 and 2), Primary Phonics,* and the *Wright Skills Decodable Books* and provided analysis of these materials at their website *www.wri-edu.org/partners.* Jenkins et al. (2003) suggested the following steps for selecting decodable materials: (1) Identify *all* of the phonics elements (letters–sounds) in the story; (2) compare the phonics elements to what your students know; (3) for independent reading select materials with known elements; (4) for assisted–instructional reading select elements that are being taught; and (5) before reading a decodable text make sure to identify the nondecodable words.

For teachers who would like to analyze their own materials, Figure 4.6 provides a checklist (Brown, 1999; Mesmer, 1999; Jenkins et al., 2003). High-quality decodable texts should list the phonics elements needed to read the book as well as nondecodable or sight words. (See Figure 4.5 for an example of such a listing with focal letter–sound patterns.) When identifying the phonics elements in a story, one should double-check the listed elements by scanning the pages of the text. Sometimes the listings fail to note difficult words in the texts. The words in texts should adhere to a scope and sequence for letter–sound instruction and should not include patterns that are more complex than the focal pattern. Decodable books should contain many known letter–sound patterns and high-frequency words. Nothing is more frustrating than sitting down with a reader and being surprised by difficult words. Unfortunately, the writers of some decodable books know very little about the developmental progression of letter–sound knowledge. For instance, the phonics book *Scooby-Doo: The Ski Lesson* (Ladd, 2005) notes on the cover that it emphasizes the *s*- blends (e.g., *st-, sl-, sp-, sm-, sk-, sc-*) but the text reads, "They were taking ski lessons! 'Skiing is a good sport!' said the teacher. 'Skiing is a scary sport,' said Shaggy." The text contains difficult patterns in the words *sport, skiing, scary.* The *r*-controlled patterns (*or, ary*), inflected ending (ing), and derivational word (ski) all present patterns that developmentally emerge *after* consonant blends (Bear, Invernezzi, Templeton, & Johnston, 2003). Therefore, the practice in reading consonant blends would be obscured by the complex vowel sounds in the words. Many phonics readers also include the target pho-

**High-quality decodable books should:**

☐ Contain a list of the specific letters–sounds and high-frequency words required to read the book.

☐ Follow a sequence for letter–sound complexity. (see Table 4.3)

☐ Include *mostly* words with learned letter–sound patterns and high-frequency words.

☐ Include individual books grouped in sets by a particular phonics element (short vowels, consonant blends, digraphs).

☐ Contain rebus pictures to represent those words that are not decodable.

☐ Contain engaging language.

**FIGURE 4.6.** A checklist for high-quality decodable text.

nics elements but then add words to the stories that do not contain these or any previously taught elements. This, of course, defeats the purpose of decodable text.

The best decodable series package books together by a defined phonics element (e.g., short vowels, blends, silent e words). Thus, Set A might include 10 books covering the short vowels and then Set B might add 10 books that integrate short-vowel knowledge with consonant blends. When teachers use sequenced sets of books, they are able to presume letter–sound knowledge presented in earlier books. The accumulation of phonics elements allows readers to build momentum. High-quality decodable texts will often use various techniques to avoid difficult patterns. Writers will select proper names that follow the focal pattern of the book, or they will use rebus pictures to add interest to stories without detracting from decodability. Importantly, high-quality decodable texts have engaging, playful language and a coherent, simple story (Stahl, Duffy-Hester, & Stahl, 1998). One of the major misconceptions about decodable text is that the language must necessarily be boring or even weird (e.g., The pig danced a jig on a fig). As Stahl et al. (1998) wrote, "It is a challenge to write texts that are both coherent and decodable but it can be done" (p. 344). High-quality decodable books have colorful pictures, letter–sound consistency, rhyming, and repetition, and all elements interact to produce a book that is engaging *and* decodable.

## Research on Decodability

Prior to 2001, very little research informed the use of decodable text, but since then, a number of new studies have advanced current knowledge (Compton, Appleton, & Hosp, 2004; Jenkins, Peyton, Sanders, & Vadasy, 2004; Juel & Roper-Schneider, 1985; Mesmer, 2001a, 2005; Vadasy et al., 2005). When exposed to decodable text, readers often tend to become stronger at decoding and tend to apply letter–sound knowledge more in their reading. The effects of decodable text, however, are mediated by the teaching context. In 1985, Juel and Roper-Schneider compared two groups of first graders, both of which were receiving the same phonics instruction. One group was reading a decodable basal, and the other was using a basal with high-frequency words. At the end of the year, both groups read words from their own basals equally well, but the decodable group was better able to decode pseudowords during the first two thirds of the year. In two smaller experiments, small groups of first graders received the same phonics instruction but read decodable or control texts (Mesmer, 2001a, 2005). Decodable groups read with more focus on the letter–sound information.

A larger experiment within a one-on-one tutoring context randomly assigned first graders to read either decodable or control texts following a phonics lesson (Jenkins et al., 2004). In this study, no differences existed between groups. The tutoring context and phonics instruction were more powerful than decodable texts. However, a subsequent experiment with tutors indicated that reading decodable text added value to phonics instruction alone (Vadasy et al., 2005). In essence, decodable text appears to strengthen decoding and add value to phonics lessons, but its impact is affected by group size and lesson content. Individual tutoring and strong phonics instruction render decodable text no better than other materials.

## Advantages and Disadvantages of Decodable Texts

When asked for their opinions about decodable text in a recent survey, K–3 teachers expressed both advantages and disadvantages (Mesmer, 2006). Primary teachers wrote, "[It is] important to reinforce letters–sounds" and "Helpful for solidifying vowels sounds." If a reader learns how to blend sounds and then finds the strategy fruitless during connected reading, he or she may abandon the strategy of using letter–sound information and resort to guessing. A second advantage of decodable text was that teachers also felt that they were helpful with beginning readers. Teachers wrote, "Useful with kindergarten students" and "The best way to start teaching reading." Decodable texts are useful with beginners because they often have enough knowledge about letters–sounds to apply their knowledge but not enough knowledge to handle the full range of variations. Decodable text may help readers transition from using only beginning sounds to fully reading words. Finally, decodable text may offer an advantage for struggling readers who are stalled developmentally. I worked with a second grader who was stuck in a pattern memorizing predictable texts. I found that using decodable text drew her attention to sounding out (Mesmer, 1999).

Teachers were equally clear about the disadvantage of this type of material. The most prominent concern was that the language of decodable texts was boring and stilted. One teacher wrote, "Most are very boring and do not use natural language." Restricting words to those that are decodable can produce texts that are colorless and unmotivating. The language can lack meaning and appeal. In addition, because the texts do require readers to exert themselves in decoding words, they can be challenging. Decoding a word is more difficult than relying on a picture or a rhyming sequence. One reader with whom I worked could read only one of these types of books each day. Finally, as with any material, decodable text should not be used exclusively. One teacher wrote, "It's helpful to have some but a steady diet would be mind numbing." Because the textual scaffolds in decodable text are so specific, it has a very specific purpose and should be used for the purpose of helping children to practice decoding.

## VOCABULARY CONTROL

Like the term *leveling*, *vocabulary control* may have both general and specific meanings. It may refer to any manipulation of the vocabulary or words in a text and thus may include decodability, repeating words, or including frequently occurring words. The *Literacy Dictionary: The Vocabulary of Reading and Writing* (Harris & Hodges, 1995) defines *vocabulary control* as "the practice of limiting the rate of introduction of new words, as in basal reading texts" (p. 275). This is the focus of vocabulary control as a textual scaffold for beginning readers. From the early part of the 20th century through the early 1980s, most basal reading series used some level of vocabulary control. If you learned to read during this time, you might have encountered a text like McKee (1966) *Tip and Mitten*. The text reads, "Find Janet, Tip. Find Janet. Janet is not here. Come Janet. Come home. Come with me. No. No Tip. Go home. Go home Tip" (pp. 22–25). Note the repetitions of words. The goal of vocabulary-controlled materials is to assist the beginning reader in acquiring a body of sight words through the repetition of words within and across stories. The primary mechanisms for support in vocabulary-controlled materials are the systematic presentation of words and a focus on words that occur frequently in English. With the repetition, readers can count on seeing new words many times within a selection. They can also count on learning the most frequently occurring words. This section describes how vocabulary-controlled materials work, identifies materials with some elements of vocabulary control, and summarizes the research on this textual scaffold. Since the mid-1980s, full vocabulary control has almost faded from beginning reading materials (Foorman et al., 2004; Hiebert, Menon, & Martin, 2005; Hiebert, 2005). However, some materials on the market contain elements of vocabulary control.

## Elements of Vocabulary Control: Instructional Pacing and Word Frequency

Vocabulary-controlled materials contain two features. First, they pace the introduction of new words within and across stories, and second, they rely on word frequency as the basis for determining word difficulty (Cunningham et al., 2005; Hiebert, 1998; Hoffman, 2002). Instructional pacing is based on within-story and across-story repetition. When authors write vocabulary-controlled materials, they introduce new words and repeat old words within the story. The vocabulary pacing in the preprimer *Tip and Mitten* part of the Reading for Meaning Series of a 1996 Houghton Mifflin basal, was very specific. In this pack was a chart providing the page on which each new word was introduced and showing the number of repetitions of the word within the book. Many pages, especially near the end of the book, contain no new words. In the first story, *Tip and Mitten* the word count is 48 (tokens) but only 10 unique words (types) make up this text. Vocabulary-controlled materials maintain tight ratios between new and total words (Hiebert, 1998; Hiebert & Mesmer, 2006). Thus, within a story, the reader encounters many words that he or she has already seen and is presented with only a few new learning words. Because of this ratio, across-story repetition must also be controlled, meaning that new words learned in a story carry over to the next story.

In an earlier era, stories within basal readers were vocabulary controlled, but now individual story books are bundled together and vocabulary controlled. For example, Book A might introduce the words *come*, *at*, and *go*, and Book B would repeat these and then introduce the new words *like* and *see*. Today publishers deliver vocabulary-controlled materials in sequenced story sets rather than bound together in a basal reader. To properly use vocabulary-controlled materials, teachers should use the stories sequentially.

The second element of vocabulary control is attention to high-frequency words. As discussed in Chapter 2, high-frequency words have been considered easier to learn. High-frequency words often serve as function words and include articles, conjunctions (e.g., *and, but*), auxillary verbs (e.g., *was, were*), and prepositions (e.g., *to, from*). Beginning readers must learn these words because the words are essential to fluent, automatic reading, but high-frequency words alone are not sufficient for skilled reading. The rich and diverse set of content words (e.g., *Hawaii, bear, sled, cookie*) carry the majority of the meaning in a text. Figure 4.7 lists the Dolch words in order, with the most frequent listed first. This list of 220 words is often used in primary grades. Other lists include *The New Instant Word List* (Fry, 1980) and *Harris–Jacobson Core Lists* (Harris & Jacobson, 1974). Vocabulary-controlled materials build text on the high-frequency words, treating words on these lists, especially the most frequent, as easier than words not on these lists. In the example of *Tip and Mitten* all but one word is within the 60 most frequently occurring words according to the Dolch list. For this reason, vocabulary-controlled texts may be particularly helpful in learning high-frequency words.

Theoretically, vocabulary-control materials encourage holistic word learning by sight. In 1921, Thorndike noted that many of the books in print for beginning readers contained high type–token ratios, requiring the reader to remember large numbers of words after very few exposures. Thorndike asserted that there needed to be a balance between new content and familiar content and that new information should receive adequate practice. He developed a word frequency book to select words with the highest utility for learners. After cataloging word frequencies, his materials systematically repeated these words for optimal practice. Gates (1926) followed with a similar word frequency book and then empirically tested his theory (Gates & Russell, 1938). His data suggested that about 35 exposures to a word would be necessary for learning. Both psychologists were significantly impressed by the gestalt approach, which focused on learning wholes as opposed to fragmented elements of stimuli.

The theories forwarded by Thorndike and Gates led to decades of holistic word learning. The famous Elson Basic Readers, known to many as the Dick and Jane readers, encouraged a word-learning practice called "look/say." Students were to look at words and simply say them and remember them using the visual image or gestalt of the words. Decoding or sounding out was not encouraged. A shift away from vocabulary control was sparked by Jeanne Chall (1967/1983), who, in her landmark book *Learning to Read: The Great Debate,* questioned whether an entire program should be based on repeating frequently occurring

| | | | | |
|---|---|---|---|---|
| the | did | know | never | ate |
| to | what | right | seven | full |
| and | so | put | eight | those |
| he | see | too | cold | done |
| a | not | got | today | use |
| I | were | take | fly | fast |
| you | get | where | myself | say |
| it | them | every | round | light |
| of | like | pretty | tell | pick |
| in | one | jump | much | hurt |
| was | this | green | keep | pull |
| said | my | four | give | cut |
| his | would | away | work | kind |
| that | me | old | first | both |
| she | will | by | try | sit |
| for | yes | their | new | which |
| on | big | here | must | fall |
| they | went | saw | start | carry |
| but | are | call | black | small |
| had | come | after | white | under |
| at | if | well | ten | read |
| him | now | think | does | why |
| with | long | ran | bring | own |
| up | no | let | goes | found |
| all | came | help | write | wash |
| look | ask | make | always | show |
| is | very | going | drink | hot |
| her | an | sleep | once | because |
| there | over | brown | soon | far |
| some | your | yellow | made | live |
| out | its | five | run | draw |
| as | ride | six | gave | clean |
| be | into | walk | open | grow |
| have | just | two | has | best |
| go | blue | or | find | upon |
| we | red | before | only | these |
| am | from | eat | us | sing |
| then | good | again | three | together |
| little | any | play | our | please |
| down | about | who | better | thank |
| do | around | been | hold | wish |
| can | want | may | buy | many |
| could | don't | stop | funny | shall |
| when | how | off | warm | laugh |

**FIGURE 4.7.** Dolch list of 220 high-frequency words in columns from most frequent to least frequent.

words. She noted that many of these words contained irregular letter–sound patterns.

Despite the long history of vocabulary control, this approach to textual scaffolding is available in very few materials today (Foorman et al., 2004; Hiebert, Martin, & Menon, 2005). One set of materials that does contain vocabulary control is the *QuickReads* series by Modern Curriculum Press. The series is designed to improve fluency within a nonfiction context. These materials, offered in second through fourth grades, contain nonfiction passages on a range of topics. Each topical section contains five passages that systematically include content-specific vocabulary while controlling passages for word frequency. A second-grade series of passages on transportation include readings on trains, bicycles, planes, and cars. Additional information is available at *www.quickreads.org*.

Although the emphasis on high-frequency words is only part of the vocabulary control equation, a number of materials focus on learning high-frequency words. These individual books are called sight words readers or high-frequency readers. The term *sight word reader* may be a bit of a misnomer. Any word, be it frequently occurring or not, can become a sight word if the reader learns it and can automatically access it by sight (Ehri, 2005). Each of these materials usually focuses on a specific set of sight words, which is listed on the cover or inside cover. In the simplest stories, only one sight word is emphasized, but the more complex stories contain several sight words. Some materials use rebus pictures to represent difficult words. Sight word readers include Scholastic's *Sight Word Readers* and *High-Frequency Readers,* Nasco's *Sight Word Readers Variety Pack,* and Rigby's *PM Starters* and *Kinderwords.* Teachers who successfully use the high-frequency readers generally send home word lists for practice, assess high-frequency word learning, and provide many other opportunities to practice these words. Like decodable readers, these are also very limited and useful for very specific purposes.

## Research on Vocabulary Control

At this time, vocabulary-controlled materials are almost nonexistent (Foorman et al., 2004; Hiebert et al., 2005). Foorman et al. (2004) analyzed six basal reading series and found that many programs presented large numbers of unique words (types) compared with total words (tokens). The total number of words in five programs ranged from about 14,000 to about 60,000 and contrasted sharply with a sixth program with about 5,500 words. The more difficult programs presented between 32 and 95 words per week, which contrasted with 15 new words that first graders in the 1980s were learning each week (Hiebert, 2002). On average, the six programs in Foorman et al.'s (2004) study contained as much as 70% of words that occurred only one time. These findings indicated that today's basals, which have the greatest opportunities to sequence stories and systematically control vocabulary, largely fail to do so.

In a survey of 362 teachers, only about 64% reported using vocabulary-controlled materials. When they did use vocabulary-controlled materials, teachers reported using them to teach high-frequency sight words (60%). Vocabulary-controlled materials are built on frequently occurring sight words and they provide practice with sight words. Teachers might also use vocabulary-controlled materials to enhance fluency (Compton et al., 2004; Hiebert & Fisher, 2002; Rashotte & Torgeson, 1985). In one study, second graders were more fluent in the vocabulary-controlled *QuickReads* than in other materials (Hiebert & Fisher, 2002). In another study, struggling students rereading materials with vocabulary control were more fluent than students rereading other materials (Rashotte & Torgeson, 1985). For fluency purposes, vocabulary-controlled materials appear to be underutilized, an interesting fact in light of the current focus on fluency.

## Advantages and Disadvantages of Vocabulary-Controlled Materials

Like other engineered formats, vocabulary-controlled materials have both advantages and disadvantages. The primary advantage of vocabulary-controlled materials is that they facilitate young readers building momentum in learning high-frequency words. Because of the instructional pacing, readers continually practice old words and gradually acquire new words until they automatically recognize them. Because of the high ratio of old words to new words, the learning is steady and hardly noticeable to the reader. The second advantage is that the structure builds confidence because readers are not constantly encountering words that they have never seen before. The consistency ensures success so that readers can feel the reward of their reading efforts. Finally, the structure may be particularly helpful for struggling learners who need continued practice to learn. The systematic approach to reading practice is exactly what struggling learners need.

Vocabulary-controlled materials also present two disadvantages. When vocabulary control was at its height, the look/say method was the primary strategy for word learning. Decoding or sounding out was not encouraged. The first major criticism of vocabulary-controlled materials was that exclusive use of high-frequency words in texts presented many irregular letters–sounds (Chall, 1967/1983). For example, the high-frequency words *the*, *to*, *he*, *you*, *of*, *was*, *said*, *they*, *what*, and *would* all contain complex letter–sound patterns that do not expose children to letters–sounds in the way that we know from spelling research they unfold developmentally (Bear et al., 2003). Spelling development tells us that children become aware of consonants, then short vowels, consonant blends, consonant digraphs, vowel digraphs, and so on (Bear et al., 2003). The second disadvantage of vocabulary-controlled materials is that the stories can be boring. Maintaining a set ratio of new to old words may support instructional pacing, but the repetition produces flat stories without rich context. To make sense of the story, the reader usually must rely on pictures. Like decodability, vocabulary control is a single-criterion material with a very specific purpose.

## SUMMARY

One important goal of beginning reading instruction is to build instructional momentum toward the acquisition of 300 to 500 words by the end of first grade (Snow, Burns, & Griffin, 1998). Each of the textual scaffolds presented in this chapter assists beginning readers in building momentum, but each does so in a distinct way. Currently, we do not have materials that comprehensively combine different textual scaffolds in beginning reading books (Foorman et al., 2004; Hiebert & Mesmer, 2006). Materials that possess one textual scaffold may not possess another. For this reason, exclusive use of a particular material might result in side effects for beginning readers. For example, qualitative leveling systems support readers with controlled word counts and language, but they do not systematically introduce high-frequency words or letter–sound information. A reader using leveled text exclusively might learn to rely only on language context but not decoding. Vocabulary-controlled texts do present high-frequency words in a systematic way, but they may discourage readers from decoding even when a word is decodable. On the other hand, decodable texts control letters–sounds, but they may distract readers from paying attention to whether their reading makes sense. In using beginning reading materials, teachers must carefully consider the needs of the reader and select texts accordingly. Chapter 6 describes how successful primary teachers have done just that.

**PART II**

# CHOOSING AND USING TEXT ANALYSIS TOOLS

# CHAPTER 5

# Choosing Text Analysis Tools
*Successful Schools*

To succeed as a team is to hold all of the members accountable
for their expertise.

—MITCHELL CAPLAN

Effective teachers know that they derive part of their strength from
working in energetic schools with dedicated leaders who build a vision
for educating students. Although a strong teacher can effect change in
her individual classroom, she can be even more influential in a strong
school. Similarly, teachers can help readers find the right books in their
classrooms, but they will be even more effective when they are supported
by a schoolwide plan for text–reader matching that is used in the
library–media center, special education classroom, reading resource
room, and bookroom. Schools can work as a team to make sure that
children all over the building are reading appropriate texts. They can
share the mission of text–reader matching and ask each person to con-
tribute important expertise to that mission. The previous four chapters
have discussed different types of text analysis tools. Not only can teachers use these tools individually, but so also can schools and grade levels.

I have included the three vignettes in this chapter because my experience with schools has shown that text analysis tools are often purchased and implemented at the building level. I have witnessed both successful and catastrophic building-level decisions. Using a text analysis
tool schoolwide has both advantages and disadvantages. A cohesive sys-

tem for understanding text difficulty is especially important when all the students and teachers in a building share a resource that impacts text–reader matching, like a bookroom or a library. Bookrooms, for instance, are not very useful without a system for communicating the difficulties of many different texts in an efficient fashion. They require the selection of a text analysis tool. A schoolwide text analysis tool can streamline communication between grade levels so that teachers can easily present materials to students. In addition, it can improve communication among principals, teachers, library media specialists, special educators, and reading specialists in ways that significantly impact readers. However, there is always a tension between order and constraint. If the text analysis tool and its use become too stringent or inflexible, then the result can be constraining to both teachers and readers. Readers who might be motivated to challenge themselves with books may not be allowed to. Teachers with knowledge and expertise at a particular grade level may disagree with the assessment of book difficulty. More often than not, when schools thoughtfully approach decisions about text analysis tools, they manage to prevent misuses and abuses of text analysis tools.

All of the schools described in this chapter possess a spirit of cooperation. They have administrators who lead their schools instructionally but also empower teachers to make decisions. With respect to text analysis tools, these schools are tenacious about children reading every day from appropriate materials. They do not compromise on text–reader matching. However, they are flexible about how to reach this goal. Schools that make the best decisions in purchasing text analysis tools do their own research before buying. They know that the educational publishing business spends enormous amounts to market its products. Companies are fighting for the attention of educators and school dollars. They want to sell their products and, toward this end, will make purchasing very convenient. Schools that successfully make decisions will not depend on text representatives and websites alone for information.

The first vignette in this chapter is about Hillcrest Elementary School and its principal, Darrell, who describes a process that his school used to make decisions about text analysis tools. Darrell's process emerged from his own administrative skills and determination to avoid expensive and ineffective products. In the second vignette, Lara, a reading specialist at Crescent Elementary School, describes a creative solution that she had for her school's bookroom. When Lara noticed that intermediate teachers were not using the bookroom she worked with them to redesign the bookroom, so that it integrated difficulty labels that were useful to both primary and intermediate teachers. The last vignette involves Janice, a media specialist at Macoby Elementary School. Janice noticed that students were often returning books that they had not read, and some students were checking out books that were not appropriate. She worked with teachers to help students find readable books. While maintaining her professional standards and ethics as a library–media specialist, she became more proactive in helping students select books.

## A PROCESS FOR MAKING DECISIONS
## (OR DARRELL'S PLAN FOR NOT GETTING RIPPED OFF)

Darrell is a principal in a rural school in a large county in the Southeast. About 75% of the students in his school receive free and reduced-priced lunch, and many live in remote rural areas. In his first year as principal at Hillcrest, Darrell was approached by a teacher who was eager to procure a particular set of math materials. The teacher lobbied Darrell and the rest of the staff to agree to the materials; however, the purchase turned out to be regretful. Darrell describes:

> "I needed to order materials because the previous administrator had not done so. In a rush to get it done, I allowed this one teacher to convince me to go with a particular set of materials. I called the rep and asked her to bring samples and it was all downhill from there. The rep was enthusiastic and convinced us that this was the best way to go. It turned out that the materials were good in one area but not so good in about five other areas. It was a rookie's mistake. I should have talked to the other teachers, asked other schools, and researched the product. But I didn't make that same mistake again."

The next purchase that Darrell's school made was books, and Darrell was ready to be more thoughtful in purchasing. As Darrell explains:

> "When we bought math materials we felt like the sales representative, who had little knowledge about our building, had told *us* what *we* needed. We decided that we were going to tell the next sales representative what we needed and we were going to be more informed about exactly what we wanted."

Hillcrest's process is described here. It emerged as the school took the necessary steps to make decisions about texts. The process included the following five steps:

- Step 1: Survey needs.
- Step 2: Establish purposes.

- Step 3: Research available materials.
- Step 4: Evaluate resources.
- Step 5: Implement the product on a trial basis.

## Step 1: Survey Needs

Hillcrest's first step was to conduct an informal survey of teacher needs. Darrell felt as though one vocal teacher had heavily influenced the decision-making process, and he wanted to get feedback from all of the Hillcrest teachers. He gathered a small committee to begin this process. The group thought that a simple, anonymous survey was a good way to start. They decided to collect information about what personnel (teachers, media specialists, special teachers) in their building needed. They wanted to be systematic and knew that the discussion about needs should involve all of the people who helped to match readers with texts. The team wanted everyone in the building to express their professional opinions honestly. They were careful not to make the survey burdensome.

To determine its needs, the Hillcrest team put together a set of questions for teachers and required all teachers to return the survey. Often schools have programs in place from previous years. The survey provided teachers an opportunity to communicate whether or not they were still using the programs without facing reproach. The Hillcrest team was sensitive to the length of the survey (two pages) and the time that teachers needed to complete it (1 week). The Hillcrest survey included the following questions:

- How do you find books for individual students? Small groups? Whole classes?
- How do you label the difficulties of books (if at all)?
- How do you know if the books are at the appropriate level?
- How do the students choose books for independent reading?
- What is most important to you when you are trying to find books for your readers?
- Do you already use some text analysis scheme in your classroom (e.g., grade levels, leveling)?
- Do you rely on publisher-provided readability levels printed on books?
- What tools do you need to better match children with texts?
- If money were no object, what tools would you like to have to help you match readers with books?
- For which readers do you have the most trouble finding books?

The Hillcrest team made sure that teachers had frequent reminders about the survey. A checklist near the survey collection point helped the team determine who had completed the questions and who had not.

Hillcrest Elementary School used a questionnaire, but in some schools this may feel burdensome. Another way to obtain information is through small focus groups. These groups consider the same questions that you might pose in a survey but answer the questions orally in a small group with a note taker. Schools often run focus groups during faculty meetings. A member of the team listens and record responses as the focus group answers questions. The disadvantage of the focus group is that some people will participate more than others. When one or two people do most of the talking, the information collected will not be representative of the entire school. Once information has been collected, the team should review and study it.

## Step 2: Establish Purposes

Sometimes a principal, a reading specialist, or a particular teacher believes that the school has a certain problem but the teachers report something slightly different. For example, in one urban school the principal observed children reading books that were too hard. She had decided that the teachers did not know how to match children with books and was on the verge of ordering an entire set of materials along with four professional development sessions. I encouraged her to gather some information from the teachers before ordering. When she did receive responses, she found that a district-level workshop had led many teachers to believe that the school district wanted children to read from their grade-level texts, even when the texts were too hard. Teachers did not need as many resources as much as they needed some freedom. After contacting the district and clarifying the policy, the principal solved the problem. Ironically, learning about how to match students with books was not the problem at all. To determine what teachers need, we must ask them.

Once the Hillcrest team collected the results, they undertook the second step: establishing the purpose for the text analysis tool that they were going to purchase. Under each question the team listed all of the responses. They made particular note of repeated comments, because these indicated convergent opinions. Hillcrest learned the importance of this step. When the Hillcrest team put together their information, they were able to narrow the field of problems to a few. They learned that, across the building, children were not easily finding appropriate texts for leisure reading or sustained silent reading. The teachers wanted a way to easily categorize trade books by difficulty. They learned that the inter-mediate-grade teachers needed to be able to assess the difficulty of sup-plementary science and social studies texts purchased for struggling readers. After surveying their teachers, Darrell and the Hillcrest team established their purpose—to find a tool that would help them evaluate the difficulty of trade books for all learners and assess the difficulty of nonfiction for struggling readers.

In setting their purposes, Hillcrest made sure to understand for whom the tool would be used. Schools making decisions should asked themselves, "Will this tool be used with struggling readers? Small groups of children? Individual readers? Beginning readers?" Some tools are well suited to beginning readers, whereas others are not. Some tools are too expensive to purchase for one or two classrooms and others are not. Although the issue did not come up with Hillcrest, school teams should consider how teachers are currently assessing students' reading levels. (Teachers at Hillcrest were using a computerized test that gives reading level in whole-grade levels and tenths.) Addressing this question is piv-otal because tools express text difficulty differently, and a school will want to find tools that coordinate with its current processes. If your school uses leveling and obtains students' reading levels using the Devel-opmental Reading Assessment, then purchasing Degrees of Reading Power makes little sense. Some text analysis tools, like Lexiles, coordi-nate with a number of widely used standardized tests. If your school administers a standardized test like the Gates–MacGinitie, you will auto-matically have access to reader Lexile levels.

Teams should also determine how ancillary components of the tool might be used. Some tools that appear to be text analysis tools actually have secondary purposes. I have seen many schools allow the quizzing components of Reading Counts and Accelerated Reader take over and become the entire focus of the tool, when it was originally purchased to facilitate text–reader matching (see the Appendix for a discussion of Reading Counts and Accelerated Reader). In many cases, abuses like these could have been curtailed if schools set parameters about the prod-ucts at the beginning.

Teachers and media specialists should carefully consider what they want the product to do. Will the tool be used primarily by teachers to identify books for instruction? Will it be used to help students locate books for themselves? Many of the newer tools contain detailed report-ing options and progress monitoring. How will the reporting options be used? The goal at this stage is to be informed about your school's needs. When schools have information about what *they* need, they are smart consumers.

## Step 3: Research Available Materials

After establishing purposes, Hillcrest began to research available tools and materials. They started by brainstorming things that they already knew about, but then each conducted a search to find other products. The word *research* means literally to re-search or to search again. Hillcrest did not trust a single source for information but searched *again* for different sources. They called friends at other schools, requested samples, printed out lists, and ordered catalogs. They also searched in professional reading journals such as *The Reading Teacher, Journal of Adult and Adolescent Literacy,* and *Language Arts* to find articles about materials. In one case, they were able to observe the materials in use. The Hillcrest team did everything they could to critically evaluate the products they were researching.

The Hillcrest team did not contact sales representatives until *after* they had conducted their research and had a list of questions ready to present. The did not rely on a sales representative to supply them with all of the information about a product. Many products and programs are expensive. Schools should consider these purchases with the same care and diligence that individuals use in purchasing cars. Once the Hillcrest team had completed its research, it prioritized the best products for each purpose.

## Step 4: Evaluating Resources

Before researching products, the team had a rough idea of the budget for the project. After their research, the team worked with Darrell, their principal, more closely to evaluate available resources. I have had teachers ask me why this process should not start with a discussion of available budget. My experience has been that schools should really understand the scope of available products, even if some are not affordable at the time. When schools limit their discussions and thinking to only products within a certain price range, they limit their knowledge. I have known schools to be so motivated to obtain the best product—and the product they want—that they will apply for grants to help them purchase it. It always helps to have a vision for your school, because the future will often present opportunities.

The word *resources,* always seems to be a polite way of saying "money." However, money is not the only important resource, especially with respect to text analysis tools. Time, books, and personnel are also important. In considering the monetary costs of a program, schools should consider incidental costs. For example, Accelerated Reader is computerized. Schools need to have the requisite computer resources and server to run the program. Schools often do not consider their current collections of books as a resource, but certain text analysis tools will prompt a need for more books. Many programs use databases, websites, or catalogs to list titles and difficulties. However, not all schools will have all of the books listed. For example, leveling resources list about 7,500 titles, but a school would not be able to obtain levels for their existing books if they are not listed in this resource. Some products will increase library circulation. Schools should assess the number of books that they have in their libraries. They should ask themselves, "If each child checked out one to two additional books per week, would we have enough? Do we have enough books at all levels?" In addition, if the library's collection is dated, then many of the titles will not be on the title lists.

Usually a tension exists between time and money. In many cases, if you are willing to invest more money, you can save time. Likewise, if you are willing to invest more time, you can save money. For example, certain programs like Lexiles and Degrees of Reading Power provide extensive lists of books. The cost is low, but the time investment is high because teachers and media specialists will need to label books. Another way to save both time and money is to coordinate text analysis tools with current assessments. Instead of purchasing a new assessment for establishing reading levels, schools should find text analysis tools that fit with the ways that *they* evaluate student reading levels. Time and money are also required for professional development. If the tool is unfamiliar, then teachers will need time to learn about it.

## Step 5: Implementing the Product on a Trial Basis

Once a decision has been made, schools often think that their work is done. What Hillcrest learned with its math materials is that the first purchase is actually a trial. If possible, schools should make a small purchase and use the tool on a trial basis. Seeing a tool and using it are quite different. When we actually use a book or program, we sometimes determine that we do not like it as much as we thought that we would. This step is the reality check. In using a new product, principals and teachers will be able to work out the kinks, examine the results of the new program, and then hone its use or decide that it does not meet expectations.

An authentic trial of a product should be consistent and in accordance with the guidelines of the program developer. Teachers are independent beings, and they will find it tempting to do it their own way. Nevertheless, if different steps are added or omitted, then no one will know if the results from the implementation are due to the deviations that individual teachers made or the actual tool itself. Teachers can actually view the implementation as an action research project. They will collect some data about their students' skill before implementing the program and then collect some data at points afterward. Throughout the implementation process, teachers should keep a brief log detailing problems, issues, and overall thoughts about the program.

Once a specific trial period is over, teachers should share their thoughts about the program. At Hillcrest, the third-grade teachers used Follett Library Resources (*www.titlewave.com*) to group their trade book collections by difficulty. They taught their students how to find appropriate books and evaluated students' oral reading accuracy before and after using the resource. They found that before using the resource only about 40% of their students were choosing appropriate books, but the number increased to 90% afterward. The intermediate teachers used Titlewave as well but found that some of the materials that they had were not listed. They discovered that they probably needed to order text sets for content areas. They also found, however, that they needed even simpler materials for their lower level readers.

Darrell describes how proud he was of his team's work: "It was a little bit of a risk for me because I was not sure that the teachers were going be as thoughtful and careful as they were. They took the whole decision-making process very seriously and worked as a team to lead the school in making a good purchase." Darrell was relieved to make effective use of his budget. He cautions readers, however, to remember that this is a longer process and that it cannot be applied to every purchase. This process offers schools a framework for making decisions about texts. Because of the many demands placed on school personnel, schools should allow 6 to 9 months, including the trial period, to apply this process. The advantage of this process is that it creates important conversations among the teachers in a building. The process also puts teachers, the ultimate users of text analysis tools, in decision-making roles.

## INTEGRATING DIFFERENT DIFFICULTY LABELS INTO THE SCHOOL BOOKROOM

Lara is a reading coach at Crescent Elementary School in the Pacific Northwest. Before becoming a reading specialist, she taught first and second grades. She served as her school's reading specialist for 3 years before assuming the role as literacy coach 1 year ago. As a Reading Recovery-trained teacher, Lara was very familiar with the leveling process and worked to set up a bookroom as soon as she became the school's reading specialist. However, as Lara explains, the bookroom was not getting used by all of the teachers in the building:

"I was so excited to set up a bookroom in my school. As a Reading Recovery teacher, I was very familiar with leveling and I bought all of the Fountas and Pinnell books to help me translate the Reading Recovery levels into units more appropriate for classroom use. At first, I set up the bookroom with books at levels A to N and then I added levels O through V in the second year. The bookroom got heavy use from the kindergarten, first-, and second-grade teachers, but I noticed that the third-, fourth-, and fifth-grade teachers were not using it as much. So, I asked a friend of mine who was a fourth-grade teacher why she wasn't using the bookroom. She told me that the letters threw her off. If she wanted a particular book in the bookroom, it was no problem to go in and get it but browsing was a little difficult. She said, 'You know, Lara, I'm not a primary person. I just don't think in all those letters. I think in third grade, fourth grade, and fifth grade. When I am just browsing through those books, I can't figure out if they are on the right level, and I get frustrated looking back and forth from the tub to the conversion chart. I have to keep picking them up and thumbing through them to try to get a feel for the difficulty.' "

At first, Lara tried a quick inservice to familiarize the intermediate teachers with the leveling system, but when this did not work she decided to reorganize the bookroom. Unwittingly, Lara had organized her school's bookroom from her own paradigm, and this paradigm was difficult for intermediate teachers. She then embarked on reorganizing the bookroom for all teachers.

Lara's first step was to decide that she would use grade-level labels for materials at third grade and higher. She explains:

"I realized that the intermediate teachers were just not familiar with the leveling system. So I used grade levels to label books. I still kept the letters but put them in parentheses, like 3.3 (N). I also created lists of the titles in the bookroom at each grade level so that the teachers would know what titles we had at their grade level."

When other teachers saw that Lara was responsive to their ideas, the first-grade team approached her about ordering some decodable readers for the bookroom. At first, the idea of *using* decodable books was a little troubling to Lara, but she wanted to respond to her teachers' needs. She created a section for decodable books and labeled the bins by the primary letter–sound focus of each book (e.g., short vowels, short vowels + consonant blends).

As Lara continued to work with teachers, she gradually added a few more labels in the bookroom. She explains how she decided when to add another label:

> "Some teachers wanted me to group titles with labels like 'science' or 'historical fiction.' Although some genres will be more difficult than others, I decided against using these kind of labels because the bookroom is organized by text difficulty and the Fountas and Pinnell leveling system addresses genre some. I try to make certain that when I add an additional label, it directly represents text difficulty, and labels like 'science' do not. I think about whether or not teachers need the label to understand the *difficulty* of the book. If I feel that the label is essential to describing the major source of support in the book, then I will use it. I keep the focus on types of support or reading levels and not content or genre. You could easily have your bookroom sliced into umpteen divisions if you didn't keep your focus."

Lara also ordered some high-interest–low-readability materials for the bookroom and labeled those. In addition, she ordered some *PM Readers* described in Chapter 4, with an emphasis on high-frequency words. The PM books are designed around the concept of vocabulary control, and Lara understood that to properly use these materials teachers must use them in sequence. So she shelved these collections together. She also put a sign by them, "Use These in Sequence," so that teachers would understand that these books should not be used interchangeably out of order. Figure 5.1 shows a diagram of the bookroom in Lara's school and Photo 5.1 shows a photograph. Note that the most prominent labels correspond with those that the teachers prefer. At grades 3 and higher, grade levels are used with Guided Reading letters in parentheses, and in kindergarten through grade 2, Guided Reading levels are used. Although Lara has built the collection over several years, she is lucky to have a supportive administrator. She also believes that creating and maintaining a well-organized bookroom actually encourages her administrator to trust her with money. Because of the time and effort that she puts into the bookroom, she proves that she is a good steward of school resources. As she explains:

> "When I first started reorganizing the bookroom it didn't feel very cohesive to me but then it was getting more use. So, I had to give up my idea of what a perfect bookroom would look like in order to make way for a usable bookroom."

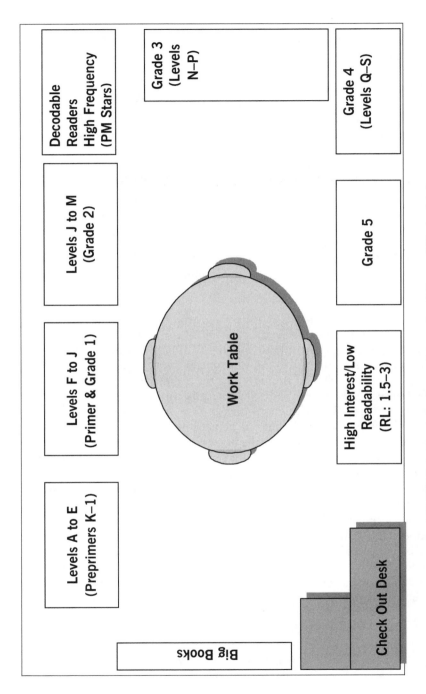

**FIGURE 5.1.** Lara's bookroom integrating different difficulty labels.

**PHOTO 5.1.** Book room.

## MAKING THE LIBRARY
## A PLACE TO FIND READABLE BOOKS

The final story is about Janice, a library–media specialist at Macoby Elementary School. Janice's school is in an urban, inner city area and serves a number of Latino students. The school houses a major English language learning program. Janice enjoys working with children from different backgrounds. She finds that the students in her school really thrill over the bright, colorful books available to them in the library, but she realized that the library could be used better. Janice explains:

> "The students in my building love coming to the library. I really work to have an open library and I want the kids to come whenever they are hungry for books. However, I wanted to find out if they were reading the books because I felt like they were just grabbing at titles with colorful covers when checkout time came. About 2 years ago, I began watching one class of third graders. I observed the books that they checked out and I began asking them as they returned the books if they enjoyed them. I might say something like, 'Maria, did you like *Junie B. Jones*? Was it a funny story?' Mostly I got empty looks and shy smiles. I realized that I needed to give them more information about how to find good books to read. So, I did a few class sessions about finding books. I talked to them about how to know if a book was too easy or too hard. I showed them where I

put the *I Can Read* books. I talked to them about the fun of reading a book that they really liked. After my little sessions things went back to the way they were. I decided to talk to the teachers. As it turned out, the teachers had noticed the same thing. They suggest labeling the difficulty of the books for the kids. I really did not like the idea. As a library–media specialist, I believe my role is to provide the entire array of materials to kids, not put up roadblocks to tell them what they can or can't read. I continued to talk to the teachers, though, because I was frustrated that the kids weren't really reading the books. I reluctantly agreed to label my fiction chapter books *on a trial basis* to see if the labels would help with the problem."

Janice used grade levels on the spines of the books based on readability. After placing the difficulty labels on the books, Janice asked the teachers to come to the library during two different class sessions to conference with students about their reading levels. Janice explained to students that each week they should try to find one book that they could read and one book at any level. Janice decided to open the library more so that the students could come back during the week and exchange books. She explained to the teachers that she would suggest the new checkout policy to students but that she would not spend her time enforcing book choices. She did not want to be in the role of telling children that they could not check out books. She also knew that she would not be able to keep the reading levels of several hundred children straight. The teachers agreed that they would help monitor book choices and guide students to finding readable books.

The result of the labeling system was very positive. Both Janice and the teachers found that the students were reading their library books much more. In conjunction with new library labels and checkout policies, teachers started to implement independent reading policies that required students to read. They also conferenced with students individually during independent reading time. (See Karen's plan for independent, self-selected reading in Chapter 7.) Janice found that she had increased the use of the library and responded to teachers' needs without compromising her principles as a library–media specialist. As she explains, she had to trust her teacher colleagues:

"When I told some of my fellow librarians what we had done at a meeting, a few of them grimaced. At first, I got a little concerned and went home in a panic thinking that I would warp these kids. When I really thought about it, I knew that really I had changed their view of the library for the better. For many students the library became a place for finding books that were readable to them as opposed to books that they couldn't access. I felt that I had maintained control over how the library used difficulty labels and that I did not compromise my beliefs. Even better, I had really worked closely with the teachers and they saw me as a part of their instructional teams, which opened the door for several other projects."

## SUMMARY

The teamwork discussed at the beginning of this chapter is the critical element in schools' successful use text analysis tools. Teachers, administrators, reading specialists, and library–media specialists who talk to each other solve problems. In each situation, as school personnel worked together, they began to trust each others' different areas of expertise. Darrell trusted his teachers to carefully research the appropriate products for the school. Lara trusted intermediate teachers, who needed a different text analysis system to make the bookroom usable, and Janice trusted the teachers in her building who believed that text difficulty labels would assist their students. Each of these professionals also possessed a core set of values that they kept central in their decision making. Lara, for instance, remained focused on the central organizing element in the bookroom: text difficulty. Janice remained focused on her role as a library–media specialist, and Darrell was focused on sharing decision making. As discussed in the Preface of this book, the educators in these schools were also willing to learn about new ways to evaluate text difficulty. Because they were knowledgeable, they were able to put text analysis tools to work for their schools.

# CHAPTER 6

# Using Text Analysis Tools

*Successful Primary Teachers*

There is a certain momentum to victory . . . and to defeat.
—BRIAN HERBERT in *Dune*

Teachers who work with beginning readers realize that this quote captures beginning reading instruction in many ways. Initial success or failure in reading instruction does produce momentum. Usually children either have a strong initial start that produces sustainable growth, or they start slowly and awkwardly and struggle for a great deal of time. In the latter case, teachers must work steadfastly to change the course for them. Finding the right books for readers is an integral part of establishing momentum. In many cases, the text–reader matching that occurs in kindergarten and first grade is so pivotal that it will produce a momentum likely toward success or toward failure. Unfortunately, text–reader matching at this stage tends to be quite complicated because readers are growing and changing rapidly and moving through many different stages.

Research indicates that teachers of beginning readers do not use one type of material exclusively (Mesmer, 2006). They seem to understand that literature, leveled texts, and decodable texts can coexist in their classrooms as they do in today's basal programs (Fooman et al., 2004; Hiebert, 2005; Hiebert et al., 2005; Hoffman et al., 2001). Teachers do not report using decodable texts in the same ways that they use vocabulary-controlled texts or qualitatively leveled texts (Mesmer, 2006). In primary classrooms, the key to using different types of materials is understanding which types of materials are most useful for which purposes.

This chapter describes four primary teachers using different types of beginning reading materials to meet the needs of their students. These teachers are fueling the kind of momentum that is essential for success. They are skilled in three respects. First, they possess basic knowledge about the many different textual scaffolds found in various beginning reading materials. They understand the distinctions among decodable texts, vocabulary-controlled texts, and qualitatively leveled texts, and they do not assume that all types of materials will present the same types of challenges to readers. Second, they deeply understand their readers and use *many* different assessments to inform their text selections. Data, rather than philosophical allegiances, dictate their choices in materials, and they choose materials that best help readers at specific developmental transitions. These teachers prioritize the needs that each reader has and select *different* texts or collections of texts to propel each reader developmentally. Third, these teachers have embraced an emerging consensus that different textual scaffolds are not inherently right or wrong but instead are right for particular needs and students and wrong for others (Brabham & Villaume, 2002; Brown, 1999; Cole, 1998; Hicks & Villaume, 2000; Mesmer, 1999).

The four vignettes in this chapter describe teachers who encounter unique problems in making text–reader matches. As they select books for their readers, they focus on developing fluent, automatic word recognition with strong comprehension. These teachers understand that the strategies their students use in reading real texts will be the strategies that stay with them. The first vignette focuses on Julie, a kindergarten teacher, who uses qualitatively leveled text in the earlier part of the year to help her emerging readers solidify their concept of word and use letter–sound knowledge in recognizing words. In the second vignette, Don, a first-grade teacher, selects decodable text to use with students who are ready to blend words and need to apply that knowledge in texts. Katherine, also a first-grade teacher, recognizes that some of her students needed the repetition and continuity of vocabulary-controlled materials to gain fluency momentum. The final vignette shows how Gina, another first-grade teacher, manages text choices within the parameters of a basal reading series. This vignette is unique in that the text–reader matching takes place within the constraints of a required basal reader, but many teachers use a basal reading series. Gina differentially uses the various basal materials and supplements when the basal materials do not meet the needs of her students. All of these teachers carefully select materials to help their learners through key developmental stages.

## USING QUALITATIVELY LEVELED TEXTS TO SOLIDIFY CONCEPT OF WORD AND LETTER KNOWLEDGE

Julie is a kindergarten teacher in a rural area. Her school serves a large geographic region, and her students often travel great distances by bus to school. Like many kindergarten teachers, Julie has students with very diverse skills. About half of her students attend Head Start in town before coming to kindergarten. For half of her class, kindergarten is their first school experience. Julie embraces an emergent view of literacy that maintains that children are developmentally adding information about print and the alphabet before they become literate in the funda-mental sense (Snow et al., 1998). However, she also recognizes the dis-parities in her class and knows that children will need differentiated in-struction even at the beginning of the year. She explains:

> "Kindergarten is changing and a lot of people do not like it. They think that assessments and standards are making kindergarten overly academic but from my perspective one of the reasons that kindergarten is changing is because the experiences that students have prior to kindergarten are changing. Kindergarten used to be the first school experience for most children but now many children come to kindergarten with rich preschool experiences. These chil-dren arrive in my classroom recognizing their names, knowing many letters, and understanding concepts like rhyming. If I am going to respond to their needs, then I will have to teach them more than the traditional kindergarten curriculum. Another group of children arrives without this knowledge. The real challenge of kin-dergarten is meeting the diverse social and academic needs of these two groups. I find that almost immediately I must have some type of differentiated instruction with small groups. I can't really just 'teach to the mean' all day."

Like most kindergarten teachers, Julie administers a set of state-required literacy measures (Oklahoma State Department of Education, 2002; Texas Education Agency, 2006; Virginia Department of Educa-tion, 2006). The assessments in Julie's state measure letter naming, ini-tial sound recognition, rhyme awareness, and concept of word. For these assessments, children attempt to name 52 upper- and lowercase letters, identify pictures that share the same initial sounds, identify pictures that rhyme, and accurately point to words in a memorized sentence. Julie administers these assessments individually and then compiles the results. She explains how the results usually look:

"Well, I always have a group of children who are low in all of the areas. These are usually children who have not been exposed to many of the concepts. Then I also have a group of children who ace the assessments and then I have a group of children who know about half of their letters, recognize some initial sounds, may hear some rhymes, but usually have a shaky concept of word."

Julie's first group of children, with depressed scores, are probably prealphabetic readers (Ehri, 2005; Ehri & McCormick, 1998; Juel, 1983). (See Chapter 4 for additional discussion.) In this phase, children use unique, arbitrary cues to help them recognize words. They do not yet understand that letters represent phonemes, or speech sounds. For instance, they might use length, double letters, pictures, or unique logos (e.g., the golden arches for McDonald's) to recognize words but they would not know that the *M* in *McDonald's* represents the /m/ sound. The third group, with knowledge of about half of their letter–sounds, are likely operating in a partial alphabetic phase. They understand that letters represent sounds and know some letters–sounds. They can use initial sounds to help them along with pictures and syntax (e.g., using the initial /j/ to recognize the word *jack-in-the-box.*). Julie's story focuses on helping children in this partial alphabetic stage.

Cal exemplifies a partial alphabetic reader. Figure 6.1 shows his results. Cal scored 39 of 52 on the letter naming. He knows many of his letters in both the upper-and lowercase forms. He also can hear some initial sounds and recognizes rhymes, but his concept of word is not solid. He has difficulty coordinating his voice with print. When children have a strong concept of word, they can accurately point to words in a line of memorized text (Morris, 1983, 1993). They understand word boundaries. Julie describes Cal's needs:

"Children like Cal are working to solidify their letter–sound knowl-edge. They have learned some letters–sounds in isolation but often these children are not exactly sure how to *use* letter–sound knowl-edge to coordinate their voice with the print. In the concept of word assessment I read them a sentence and point to the words and they have to read and point. Kids with partial knowledge like Cal will experience some confusion in accurately pointing to words as they repeat sentences. They may get one sentence but they usually get confused when they come to multisyllable words, and they are often not able to locate words within sentences. My instructional goals with children like Cal are to review and strengthen their letter knowledge and to give them practice with accurate finger pointing."

**LETTER NAMING**

**Uppercase**

| | | | | | | |
|---|---|---|---|---|---|---|
| O | H [I] | S | E | G | P | |
| X [K] | V | I | M | J [I] | D | K |
| Y | T | W | Z | U | A | L |
| B | Q | R | C | F | N | |

Total: 23/26

**Lowercase**

| | | | | | | |
|---|---|---|---|---|---|---|
| b [d] | x | e [c] | c | j | m [n] | |
| l | u | r [n. r.] | t | q [b] | h | y [n. r.] |
| s | d [n. r.] | o | a | k [n. r.] | w [n. r.] | |
| i | p [n. r.] | v | f | n | z | g |

Total: 16/26

[n. r.] = no response

---

**CONCEPT OF WORD**

| | Pointing | | Finding words | |
|---|---|---|---|---|
| 1     2 | | | | |
| The cat sits by the tree. | 1 | *cat* | 1 | *tree* 1 |
| 1   2 | | | | |
| She sees a bird. | 0 | *She* | 1 | *sees* 0 |
| 1   2 | | | | |
| The cat chases after the bird. | 0 | *chases* | 0 | *after* 0 |

Total: 4/9

---

**INITIAL SOUNDS**

| | | | | | | |
|---|---|---|---|---|---|---|
| O | H | S | E | G | P | |
| X | V | I | M | J | D | K |
| Y | T | W | Z | U | A | L |
| B | Q | R | C | F | N | |

Total: 13/26

---

**RHYMING**

**Child produces a word or nonsense word that rhymes with the two targets.**

1. tree–me   bee    5. no–sew   toe
2. hi–guy   nice    6. nap–cap   sap
3. rig–pig   hig    7. rope–hope   bowl
4. head–bed   red    8. hop–mop   top

Total: 6/8

**FIGURE 6.1.** Cal, an emergent reader developing concept of word.

Julie understands what research has confirmed: Concept of word is an essential insight for beginning readers and is bolstered by letter–sound and phoneme knowledge (Morris, 1983, 1993; Morris, Bloodgood, Lomax, & Perney, 2003). She likes to use qualitatively leveled books for concept of word practice. As educators have established, leveled texts contain repetitive, memorable sentences that rely on language structures characteristic of young children (Clay, 1993; Cunningham et al., 2005; Peterson, 2001). Julie begins by using the caption books with only one or two words per page that name the pictured item. *I Get Dressed* is a good example. The text of this book reads, "My pants. My shirt. My socks. My boots." She explains:

> "My students can use the pictures to help them remember the words and can point to the two words on the page. I try to limit the number of words that have more than one syllable."

When children are just learning concept of word, they will often think that each syllable represents a word, so when they come to a sentence like "Peas porridge hot," they will get confused in their pointing. They will say the word *hot* when they encounter the second syllable of the word *porridge*. After using caption books, Julies moves on to books with repetitive sentences with no multisyllable words. *Ice Cream* (Cowley, 1986) is an example of a slightly more advanced leveled book. The print reads, "We like ice cream in the car. We like ice cream in the plane. We like ice cream in the snow." This book adds more words to each page but does not add syllables. Then Julie uses books with single sentences and multisyllable words at the final sentence position. *I Am* (Cutting, 1988) is a good example of this kind of book, "I am eating. I am drinking. I am reading. I am writing." When children can accurately point to words in these books, she moves to books that have multisyllable words in many positions. For example, *Books* (Cutting, 1988) reads, "I read about ghosts. I read about space ships."

When they are developing letter–sound skills and concept of word, children need some type of support that will help them remember words in text. They often are not reading in the traditional sense, but they benefit from using text to coordinate their voices with print. As Julie explains:

> "The features of these simple leveled books really scaffold voice–print matching because the books can be selected at increasingly difficult levels. I move from books that contain one to two words per page to those with single-syllable words in a single sentence per page to those containing single sentences on a page but some

| Text Feature | Title |
|---|---|
| **A. Caption Books** (1–2 words representing a picture) | *Little Brother* (Cowley, 1986) *Building Blocks* (Cutting, 1988) *What's in This Egg?* (Cutting, 1988) *The Barbeque* (Cutting, 1988) |
| **B. One sentence/page and no multisyllable words** | *Ice Cream* (Cowley, 1986) *Our Grand Dad* (Cutting, 1988) *Down to Town* (Cowley, 1986) |
| **C. One sentence/page and a multisyllable word in the final position** | *I Am* (Cutting, 1988) *At School* (Cutting, 1988) *The Long, Long Tail* (Cowley, 1986) *I Like* (Cutting, 1988) *Faces* (Cutting, 1988) |
| **D. One sentence/page and multisyllable words throughout the sentence** | *I'm Bigger Than You* (Cowley, 1987) *Books* (Cutting, 1988) *Bubbles* (Depree, 1988) |

**FIGURE 6.2.** Julie's text set for developing concept of word.

multisyllable words. By the time children get to the last set of books they are solid in concept of word and know a few common sight words. This process usually only takes a couple of weeks."

Julie's text set for developing concept of word is listed in Figure 6.2.

## USING DECODABLE TEXTS TO DEVELOP BLEND WORDS IN CONTEXT

Don is a first-grade teacher and 25-year veteran teacher who has worked in both parochial and public schools in the Northeast. He currently teaches in an elementary school in Manhattan serving a multicultural population of recent immigrants. Most of his students are children of working-class parents. Don uses his own collection of assessments that he has honed over the years. He administers the assessments at the beginning of the year, in January, and in May. The beginning-of-the-year assessments include letters–sounds; a phonological awareness assessment measuring rhyming, initial sounds, blending, and segmenting; a word list; and the Primary Spelling Inventory (Bear et al., 2003). In January and May he administers an informal reading inventory as well.

Don describes how and when he uses decodable text:

"I started teaching in 1981 in a small parochial school. We used the Lippincott Series, which was called a linguistic basal but it would be called decodable today. After using it about 3 years, I felt that it was really good for the first 3–4 months of first grade and then after that outlived its usefulness and got boring for the kids. I was delighted, in the early 1990s, when whole language came around. I was taking graduate classes to get a master's degree in reading and all the rich literature was great. At the time, I was still teaching in the parochial school and I converted totally to using authentic literature and Little Books in my classroom. In 1997, I took my current job because I wanted a challenge with a new population. However, I found that starting out with materials like the Little Books (leveled text) and literature did not work with my kids. The kids just seemed to rely on guessing. I think that it worked in my previous school because I had had a lot of parent support and the kids would practice at home. In my new job I decided that I needed to try something more like the Lippincott series to get the kids going. At the time I did it on the sly because people were really against using those kinds of materials. I remember going to the bookstore and buying a bunch of packs of *Bob Books* (Maslen & Maslen, 1999). I would use them for a couple of months to get the kids to blend words and then I would pull in more literature. Now there are more available and it's not such a stigma to have them in your classroom."

Don uses decodable texts for readers needing very specific skills. Sandeep is a good example of a reader benefiting from decodable text. Figure 6.3 shows his assessment results. Note that Sandeep knows 24 of 26 letters–sounds and has a strong concept of rhyming and initial sounds. He can also blend sounds orally and segment some sounds. His spelling test indicates that he has a solid understanding of beginning and ending consonants and occasionally includes vowels in his spellings, although not always accurately. Sandeep is beginning to show what researchers have called "full alphabetic" behaviors (Ehri, 2005). During this phase, readers are able to blend sounds in words together, paying particular attention to vowels. Don explains why he uses decodable text with readers at this stage:

"I have found that I can get kids blending sounds together in isolated words, but if I give them a book with a lot of variation in the vowel sounds, the kids will just abandon decoding altogether. For example, if I am trying to teach the short-\o\ sound and then I give the

```
SPELLING TEST
Word                Child's spelling
  1.  bag           bg
  2.  fin           fn
  3.  ten           ten
  4.  rob           rb
  5.  nut           nut
  6.  hole          l
  7.  bait          bt
  8.  slap          su
  9.  stem          m
 10.  sheep         hp
```

```
INITIAL SOUNDS
Child says a sound or word that begins with the letter. Short-vowel sounds
are used for vowels.
O    H    S    E    G    P
X    V    I    M    J    D    K
Y    T    W    Z    U    A    L
B    Q    R    C    F    N
Total: 24/26
```

## PHONEMIC AWARENESSS

### RHYMING
Child produces a word or nonsense word that rhymes with the two targets.

| | | | | | | |
|---|---|---|---|---|---|---|
| 1. | tree–me | see | 5. | no–sew | glow |
| 2. | hi–guy | sky | 6. | nap–cap | sap |
| 3. | rig–pig | dig | 7. | rope–hope | nope |
| 4. | head–bed | red | 8. | hop–mop | top |

Total: 8/8

### BLENDING
Child blends the sounds together to make a word.

| | | | | | | |
|---|---|---|---|---|---|---|
| 1. | s-a-t | sat | 5. | sh-e-d | shed |
| 2. | h-u-m | hum | 6. | l-u-m-p | lup |
| 3. | i-t | it | 7. | t-a-ke | take |
| 4. | s-t-o-p | stop | 8. | r-u-n | run |

Total: 7/8

### SEGMENTING
Child breaks each word into the individual sounds.

| | | | | | | | | |
|---|---|---|---|---|---|---|---|---|
| 1. | at | /a/ /t/ | 1 | 5. | big | /b/ /i/ /g/ | 1 |
| 2. | nap | /n/ /a/ /p/ | 1 | 6. | slap | /sl/ /a/ /p/ | 0 |
| 3. | bet | /b/ /e/ /t/ | 1 | 7. | nod | /n/ /o/ /d/ | 1 |
| 4. | mug | /m/ /u/ /g/ | 1 | 8. | ship | /sh/ /i/ /p/ | 1 |

Total: 7/8

**FIGURE 6.3.** Sandeep, a reader ready for decodable text.

kids a book with words like *boil*, *shook*, or *cork*, they are going to get derailed. I need books that I can pick up and know that they will have short 'o' words for practice so that the kids can apply their blending skills. Adults get so worked up about these materials, but the kids love feeling that they can do it and that they are really reading. Kids get a sense of accomplishment from working out words that they have not necessarily seen before in print."

In addition, research indicates that the process of using grapheme–phoneme connections actually facilitates reader's retaining words in memory (Ehri, 2005; Snow et al., 1998).

Don uses decodable text with groups of students who know almost all of their letters–sounds and especially their vowel sounds. These children tend to use consonant sounds in spellings and may occasionally include some vowels. Don has picked up on what research tells us about phonemic segmentation; it is highly related to decoding and, in fact, estimates decoding potential (Nation & Hulme, 1997; Muter & Snowling, 1998). Decodable text is useful for children who are primed to apply letter–sound knowledge but have not acquired the many variant vowel spellings in English. Don explains:

> "There is no way to teach kids all of the vowel patterns before you put books in their hands. And if you give them books with a mix of all kinds of complex vowel patterns, then you might as well not teach kids to use letter–sound knowledge. They will not use what they know in text, because they can't."

Don is quick to point out that his use of decodable text now is quite different from his first experience with the Lippincott basal. The Lippincott basal was fully decodable throughout the first-grade year. As Don sensed initially, most readers really only need this type of material for a few months when they are trying to decode fully (Juel & Roper-Schneider, 1985). He recognizes that a diet of decodable text exclusively can get monotonous. He explains:

> "I usually use the decodables for about 2 to 3 months. Once the kids have a solid set of sight words, a command of short vowels, consonant blends, digraphs, and silent-*e* patterns, I rely on other materials and eventually move toward using the *I Can Read* literature."

In Don's classroom, most of the class will use decodable texts from September through December, but not all children will be at the same point developmentally. Some children will simply not be ready for this type of material, whereas others will have already surpassed the point at which this might be useful.

## USING VOCABULARY-CONTROLLED MATERIALS TO ENHANCE FLUENCY

Katherine is also a first-grade teacher, but she teaches a very different group of children. Her students live in the suburbs of a large city in the Pacific Northwest and have a great deal of home support. Many of them enter first grade with reading skills. Katherine explains:

> "Many of the children with whom I work are already beginning readers. They have a base of 50 or more words that they know automatically by sight and they have been practicing reading all year long. When I changed schools I wasn't sure exactly what to do with these kids. By January they could do what my previous classes were doing in May."

Katherine's school uses fluency-based oral reading norms to track the progress of students. Katherine explains how these fluency measures assisted her in choosing materials for her students:

> "Before I came to Princeville Elementary School, I had never heard of doing fluency measures. I almost laughed out loud when I went to the training and they told us that we had to time the students reading with stopwatches. It just seemed really strange, but there were some things that I picked up on with some of my students that I never would have known without the fluency measures. In first grade we conduct fluency assessments in January and May. We have three passages for each time, and we time the students reading each passage for 1 minute and then record the number of words that they read correct per minute. We use their middle score (of the three passages) and compare it with a set of local guidelines to see if they are on track. After doing this for the first time, one January I realized that several of my students needed fluency work. I had thought that they were doing fine when, in fact, they were below in fluency. I had really been operating with this mind-set that getting the kids accurate was my goal in first grade. I hadn't been thinking about fluency."

For January, the benchmark was 23 words correct per minute and for May the score was 53 words correct per minute (Hasbrouck &

Tindale, 1992). Benchmark scores represent the minimum number of words correct per minute that a student should read. Students who do not meet these benchmarks are considered at risk and are often provided with additional help. (Teachers who use the Dynamic Indicators of Basic Early Literacy Skills, Texas Primary Reading Inventory, or Reading Naturally program can obtain similar fluency data on their students.)

One of Katherine's students, Heather, read 15 words correct per minute (wcpm) in January. Katherine describes trying to find materials for her:

> "I was a little surprised about Heather because she was such a sweet little girl and she was accurate. I had always thought her to be methodical and careful, but really she needed to be more fluent."

Katherine decided that Heather needed a lot more reading practice and some work with high-frequency words, but she struggled with finding materials. Katherine began using leveled texts but soon grew frustrated because Heather did not seem to be improving.

> "I would listen to her read orally and on the sly would just look at the clock to estimate the number of words correct per minute that she was reading. It just didn't seem to go up. I realized that she was confronting too many difficult and unfamiliar words when she was reading. I felt that she needed more continuity."

Katherine wanted to use materials that repeated words within and across passages. As described in Chapter 4, these materials are called "vocabulary controlled." Katherine began by looking for old basal readers and located one in the back of her reading specialist's closet. It was published in 1980. After reviewing the book to confirm that the words in stories did systematically build, Katherine asked Heather to read one story each day to a partner and then take the story home and read it to her mother. The next day Heather would read the story for a third time to Katherine before the start of school. By the middle of March, Heather was reading 44 wcpm and approaching the benchmark of 53 wcpm. Katherine describes how she added other materials designed to improve fluency:

> "The old basal ran out in about 3 weeks. By that time I had already talked my reading specialist into ordering the Rigby PM Stars. I also used the older *I Can Read* titles like *Little Bear* (Minarik, 1957). You can't use the newer ones because the numbers on the front

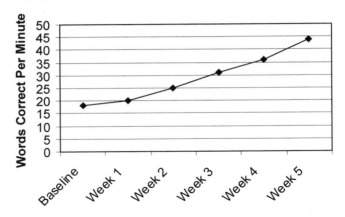

**FIGURE 6.4.** Heather's improvement in fluency with vocabulary-controlled materials.

mean absolutely nothing. I found that the older *I Can Read* books really helped her develop fluency."

Figure 6.4 shows Heather's improvement in fluency as measured by words correct per minute. Katherine's work with Heather is supported by the work of teachers like Cole (1998), who found that struggling readers enjoy and flourish with the consistency of the *I Can Read* series. In the Randall and Carol White Reading and Math Center at Oklahoma State University, we have had similar results with even shorter intervention times. Research has also supported the theory that materials with vocabulary control do, in fact, enhance fluency (Hiebert & Fisher, 2002). Like decodability, vocabulary control helps students to reach a threshold of performance. Once they have fulfilled their purposes, vocabulary-controlled materials would be replaced by other, more authentic materials.

## BALANCING BASAL RESOURCES

A 2006 survey showed that about 50% of primary teachers were required to use a basal reading series but could supplement as they wished (Mesmer, 2006). Gina, working in an urban district in the South, is a representative of these teachers. She describes the requirements:

"Our district is kind of middle of the road. We have to use the basal and report progress quarterly on the basal unit tests. However, we have some autonomy in how we use it. We use Macmillan. We can select from the materials in the basal package and we can add materials. For each 1-week unit we have the student anthologies, which are the hardback readers, about three individual leveled books, a big book, and a black-and-white phonics practice reader. In the anthology there is also a phonics poem. We do not use the workbooks but occasionally use the backline masters."

Gina realized that the basal offered many textual options but that she had to decide how to use them. This situation is relatively new, because basals in earlier years typically used only one format (e.g., decodable, literature, or vocabulary controlled) and did not require teachers to negotiate among different text types. Gina's first step was to negotiate which materials in the basal were essential. She explains:

"The most difficult thing for me was figuring out which materials everyone needed to have some exposure to. Basically you couldn't possibly use everything. If I used the basal exactly as the directions told me, my children would be overwhelmed and so would I. I decided that I liked the theme-related units and would use them to ground my instruction but would add or subtract materials. I wanted everyone in the class to be exposed to the big book, anthology selection, and anthology poem for each unit. The children needed these selections to be ready for the unit tests and our class word study (phonics)."

Gina's second step was to address another very common problem:

"I knew that the anthology selections would be too difficult for a group of children. I wanted these children to be exposed to anthology selections but these selections would not suffice for all children's reading practice, especially at the beginning of the year."

Gina was committed to making sure that every child in her class read appropriate materials daily. Although she supported her struggling readers in rereading the anthology selections, she also supplemented them with easier books. Gina used flexible groups that changed quarterly based on the unit tests and her observations. So the groupings of children were not stagnant. Figure 6.5 lists the materials that Gina used for whole-group and differentiated instruction.

For whole-group instruction, Gina read the basal materials and some supplemental materials aloud. She also asked students to reread the anthology selections individually or in small groups. She supple-

| | | Basal Text Selections and Supplemental Materials | | | |
|---|---|---|---|---|---|
| **Teaching context** | **Mon.** | **Tues.** | **Wed.** | **Thur.** | **Fri.** |
| **Whole group (shared reading)** | Big-book selection | Big-book selection (reread and word work)<br><br>Anthology story | Anthology story (with word work) | *Supplement*: Theme-related literature with vocabulary–comprehension instruction | *Supplement*: Theme-related literature (continued from Thursday) with vocabulary–comprehension instruction |
| **Small group** | Anthology poem | Anthology story | On-level students: Leveled readers<br><br>Lower-level students: Anthology poem and story (reread) | | |
| **Individual practice** | On-level and lower-level students: Anthology poem | On-level students: Phonics practice readers<br><br>Anthology story<br><br>Lower-level students: *Supplement: Bob Books* | On-level students: Leveled readers<br><br>Lower-level students: Anthology poem<br><br>Anthology (listening)<br><br>*Supplement: Bob Books* | *Supplement*: Student self-selected reading (individuals read for the teacher) | *Supplement*: Student self-selected reading (individuals read for the teacher) |

**FIGURE 6.5.** Gina's weekly plan for using and supplementing the text selections in her basal reading series.

mented her whole-group instruction each week by reading aloud a theme-related literature selection. Gina felt that the basal needed stronger vocabulary and comprehension instruction:

> "The stories at the beginning of the year are too short to do much comprehension and vocabulary instruction with and I refuse to sit around thinking up dozens of inane activities for a story like *Max, the Cat* (Morris, 2003). I would rather read a meatier story to the children and ask them to do meaningful vocabulary and comprehension work with it."

Gina recognizes what long-time vocabulary researchers know: The words that children can read in grade 1 will not be rich from a vocabulary standpoint (Biemiller, 2006; McKeown & Beck, 2003).

For differentiated instruction, Gina used a combination of both basal materials and supplements. Gina asked students to read daily in small groups and individually. One aspect that makes Gina's choice of instructional materials unique is that she provides a number of different materials for reading practice. From the basal she uses the phonics practice readers and the leveled books. She supplements these with simpler decodable and leveled texts for her lower level readers. In addition, she also provides literature for on- and above-level readers:

> "In September and October my above- and on-level readers can usually pick up the phonics readers and read them independently. Once they get the hang of blending sounds together, they can do it. But my lower-level readers need shorter decodables and leveled texts. By November my stronger readers need more practice books because they end up whipping right through both the phonics readers and leveled books offered by the basal. They are really ready for more literature."

Today's basal readers are much more diverse than they have been in previous years. They include many different text formats. Nonetheless, as Foorman et al. (2004) have noted, there are few directions about how to use materials within basal reading series. Gina has learned how to negotiate her district's requirements and the offerings in her basal reading series. She prioritizes both the essential selections in the basal as well as essential instructional goals (even if they are not well addressed in her basal reading series). Instructionally, she is committed to extending the basal to meet comprehension and vocabulary goals for her readers. Gina is also committed to ensuring that each of her students practices reading every day. Because she knows that the basal reading series will not fully address her goals, she supplements for particular instructional purposes and readers.

## SUMMARY

For primary teachers, making appropriate text choices for readers is one of the most challenging jobs. The text–reader match is challenging because beginning readers are diverse and they move through many different phases within a few short years. As illustrated, students in the first grade can have very different needs at different times. At this time, the textual offerings in the primary classroom are diverse so that they can mirror the diversity of instructional needs in the primary classroom. What the teachers in this chapter all possess is cognitive flexibility, or the ability to coordinate multiple mental representations in tandem (Cartwright, in press; Sinott, 2002). The teachers in these vignettes coordinate information about many different types of texts with information about many different types of readers. They are able to take the perspective of beginning readers and understand how these students will respond to a text. In addition, these teachers are able to work within the realities of today's classroom. They understand that there are no perfect textual solutions but instead better textual solutions. They negotiate what their students need, what districts are requiring, and what they have available. They monitor the materials that their students are reading and do not persist in text choices that are ineffective. Teachers like Gina, Don, Katherine, and Julie understand their roles in launching beginning readers and know that the text–reader match is integral to sustaining momentum.

# CHAPTER 7

# Using Text Analysis Tools
*Successful Intermediate Teachers*

Reading is to the mind what exercise is to the body.
—SIR RICHARD STEELE

Most good intermediate teachers know that, although students may arrive in their classrooms with the ability to read, they must maintain and strengthen their reading muscles during the third through fifth grades. Text analysis tools are instrumental in enabling the reading workout, but often they are not used. The purpose of this chapter is to illustrate how four teachers in grades 3 through 5 have used text analysis tools to help them achieve the important task of text–reader matching. Although each story is unique, there are several recurring themes. First, all of the teachers described in this chapter understand the importance of book matching. They treat this instructional essential with urgency and gravity by making changes when materials are not appropriate. Second, the teachers in these vignettes accept that all the students in their classrooms will not be reading the same materials all the time. They do not expect to use the same materials instructionally for all students, and they differentiate their text choices. Third, the teachers in these vignettes know that they must have a way to assess the difficulty of books quickly and efficiently. They understand that text analysis tools help them do their jobs better. Nonetheless, these teachers do not use text analysis tools exclusively. They talk with their students, assess, reassess, and observe. They know that tools are imperfect, and they accept the limitations of the text analysis tools.

The first story describes how Karen, a third-grade teacher, has used informal reading inventories to improve text–reader matching during the independent, self-selected reading of her Four-Blocks classroom (Cunningham, Hall, & Defee, 1991). She has organized her classroom collection so that her students can find books to read. The second vignette details David's process for analyzing selections for classroom novel studies. The vignette shows how David made sure that all of the students in his fifth-grade class were reading appropriate literature during novel studies. The third vignette illustrates how Rosa, a fourth-grade teacher, uses text analysis tools to communicate with parents. She uses text analysis tools to help parents select appropriate materials for gift giving and summer reading. In the fourth vignette, Cheryl describes how she located high-interest, low-readability materials for struggling intermediate readers served in a resource room. All of these vignettes show how teachers integrate multiple pieces of data to facilitate optimal matches between readers and texts.

## FACILITATING SELF-SELECTED READING USING TEXT ANALYSIS TOOLS

Karen is a third-grade teacher in an urban school in the Southwest. Most of her students receive free or reduced-price lunch and have parents who are working two or more jobs. When Karen first began teaching third grade, she quickly learned that she could not assume that her students would be able to read the standard third-grade textbooks and children's literature that she was planning to use.

Karen uses the Four-Blocks organizational structure (Cunningham et al., 1991). The Four-Blocks plan is a multilevel, multimethod organization of the reading–language arts block. Four-Blocks teachers divide the reading time into four sections: Guided Reading (teacher facilitated), Working with Words (phonics and vocabulary), Writing, and Self-Selected Reading. During the self-selected reading time, students spend about 30 minutes reading materials at their independent levels. As Karen explains, this was problematic at the beginning:

> "I remember my first year teaching. I had filled my book corner with third-grade standards like, *Stuart Little, The BFG, Encyclopedia Brown, Ramona,* and *Tales of a Fourth Grade Nothing.* For the first 4 weeks of school, I thought that I would pull my hair out during self-selected reading. Nobody was reading. People were pretending to read, changing books constantly, whispering behind book covers, and passing notes. Initially, I thought it was a behavior issue

and then I realized it was an instructional issue. My kids weren't reading because the books were too hard. I learned that if my kids were going to read at all, I would have to do two things: learn more about their reading levels and examine my collection."

Karen's experience reflects what can happen during sustained silent reading if careful monitoring and supports are not provided to students (Kelley & Claussen-Grace, 2006; Lee-Daniels & Murray, 2000). In her intermediate classroom, Kelley (2006) noticed students "fake reading," not paying attention to the content of their reading, and taking numerous water and bathroom breaks. Lee-Daniels and Murray (2000) also reported students scanning pages, changing books, and indicating boredom during DEAR (Drop Everything and Read) time. Observant teachers like Karen and the aforementioned teachers can remedy implementation problems with independent reading and convert reading into a powerful activity. Karen developed a plan to improve text–reader matches for self-selected reading. The plan included four steps: (1) determining students' reading levels; (2) selecting and labeling books for self-selected reading; (3) conducting individual conferences; and (4) reevaluating reading levels.

Karen's plan was not complex. Her first step was to obtain information about her students' reading levels. Every September, Karen administers the Classroom Reading Inventory (Silvaroli & Wheelock, 2004) to each student in her class. (See the box on p. 132 for other informal reading inventories [IRIs].) This assessment gives a basic estimate of the three reading levels for each student: independent, instructional, and frustrational levels. For the Classroom Reading Inventory, the independent level is that at which the student can read without help (98–100% word accuracy with 90% comprehension). Most of the students' independent, self-selected reading material should come from this level. The instructional level is that at which the student can function with assistance from the teacher (95% word accuracy with 75% comprehension). The frustrational level is the level at which materials are too difficult even with help (< 90% word accuracy and < 50% comprehension). Figure 7.1 shows Karen's class by reading levels. For the purposes of estimating reading levels for self-selected reading, Karen orders the list by the highest independent level for each child at the beginning of the year. The list shows that in September many of her students read independently at the second-grade level or lower. In fact, some children read independently at first grade. A few students read independently at or above grade 3. Figure 7.1 also shows that for some children no instructional level was found. This sometimes occurs with IRIs. When no instructional level is identified, a student is proba-

## A LIST OF COMMON INFORMAL
## READING INVENTORIES

Informal reading inventories (IRIs) contain graded passages with questions. The student reads the passage and then answers the accompanying questions. From an IRI teachers can estimate students' independent, instructional, and frustrational reading levels. IRIs differ in their emphases or features, but all have the same format.

- Woods, M. L. J., & Moe, A. J. (2006). *Analytical Reading Inventory, 8th edition.* Columbus, OH: Merrill Prentice Hall.
- Johns, J. (2005). *Basic Reading Inventory: Preprimer to twelfth grade, 9th edition* Dubuque, IA: Kendall/Hunt.
- Silvaroli, N. J., & Wheelock, W. H. (2004). *Classroom Reading Inventory, 10th edition.* Boston: McGraw-Hill.
- Applegate, M. D., Quinn, R. B., & Applegate, A. J. (2007). *The Critical Reading Inventory: Assessing students' reading and thinking, 2nd edition.* Columbus, OH: Merrill Prentice Hall.
- Ekwall, J. L., & Shanker, E. E. (1999). *Ekwall/Shanker Reading Inventory, 4th edition.* Boston: Allyn & Bacon.
- Morris, D. (2005). *The Howard Street Tutoring Manual, 2nd edition.* New York: Guilford Press.
- Burns, P. C., & Roe, B. D. (2001). *Informal Reading Inventory: Preprimer to twelfth grade, 6th edition.* Boston: Houghton Mifflin.
- Flynt, E. S., & Cooter, R. B. (2004). *Reading Inventory for the Classroom, 5th edition.* Columbus, OH: Merrill Prentice Hall.
- Stieglitz, E. L. (2002). *The Stieglitz Informal Reading Inventory, 3rd edition.* Boston: Allyn & Bacon.
- Leslie, L., & Caldwell, J. A. (2005). *Qualitative Reading Inventory, 4th edition.* Boston: Allyn & Bacon.

bly transitioning from one level to the next. Karen commented about the independent levels of her students:

> "When I first used the IRI, I was a bit shocked and depressed to find so many students who could not read independently at the third-grade level. Then I reminded myself that in September they had just finished *second* grade and that they had not been in school for 3 months. Also, I knew that they never would read at the third-grade level if they were constantly frustrated with materials that were too difficult."

| Student | Independent | Instructional | Frustrational |
|---|---|---|---|
| Tagliera, Bryce | Preprimer | Primer | 1 |
| Rodriguez, Juan | Primer | 1 | 2 |
| Smith, Shamira | Primer | 1 | 2 |
| Divorti, Gibson | 1 | 2 | 3 |
| Eggleston, Tina | 1 | 2 | 3 |
| Taylor, David | 1 | 2 | 3 |
| Ramirez, Cassidy | 1 | 2 | 3 |
| Felton, Tavon | 1 | 2–3 | 4 |
| Adams, Kay | 2 | | 3 |
| Lewis, Trey | 2 | | 3 |
| Hamm, Keisha | 2 | 3 | 4 |
| Kelly, Tammy | 2 | 3 | 4 |
| Bremen, David | 2 | 3 | 4 |
| Williams, Bailey | 2 | 3 | 4 |
| Price, Taylor | 2 | 3 | 4 |
| Metz, Dione | 2 | 3 | 4 |
| Hutchens, Claire | 2 | 3 | 4 |
| Dannon, Cayley | 3 | 4 | 5 |
| Jordan, Anita | 4 | 5–6 | 7 |
| Smith, LaShay | 5 | | 6 |

**FIGURE 7.1.** Karen's class by reading levels on the Classroom Reading Inventory.

Karen realized that if students were to become strong, fluent readers, they must read materials at the appropriate levels, even if those levels did not coincide with their grade levels.

Karen's second step was to evaluate her classroom library and label the books that would be available for self-selected reading. To get a feel for the proportion of her students reading at different levels, Karen organized groups of students by their highest independent reading levels (see Figure 7.1). The list showed that about 40% of the students were reading independently at or below the first-grade level and about the same percentage were reading at the second-grade level. She observed:

> "IRI data showed me that I needed to align my collection with a high proportion of students reading at lower grade levels, especially at the beginning of the year. Originally, I had organized my collection with mostly grade 3 books but I needed more first- and second-grade books."

Starting first with her existing collection, Karen devised a labeling scheme. She explained:

> "The first time I labeled it took me about 2 hours. I had about 75 books and I had to sit in front of the computer, type the book title into the website (*www.titlewave.com*), and put the level on the book. [Titlewave is a listing of books with difficulties in Lexiles and grade levels.] Then I wrote the grade level in small numbers inside the back cover, then I wrote it on a Post-it Note that I stuck to the book. I decided that I would code the spine of each book in my classroom library based on the difficulty. I wrote the levels inside the covers because I didn't want to have to redo my work if the labels fell off the books. After I got the reading levels, I devised a coding system for the students to use. I was afraid that the numbers would encourage competition, so I used colors and put dots on the spines of the books."

Although some books already provided estimates of reading level, Karen opted to use one consistent source to estimate difficulty so that the books could be equivalently compared. She labeled most books in half-year increments using colors. Figure 7.2 shows her system. The color system also has a built-in mnemonic for her. She made the lighter colors, like white and yellow, correspond with the easier books because easier books are "lighter reading." As the books become more difficult, the colors get deeper. The mnemonic helps when she is moving around the classroom or when the chart is not visible. Karen knows without looking that a yellow book will be easier than a red book, which will be

| Book Reading Level | Color | Sample Title |
|---|---|---|
| PP-P | White | *Inside, Outside, Upside Down* |
| 1.0–1.9 | Yellow | *Poppleton Everyday* |
| 2.0–2.4 | Orange | *Cam Jansen and the Mystery of the Gold Coins* |
| 2.5–2.9 | Red | *The Chalk Box Kid* |
| 3.0–3.4 | Green | *Boxcar Children* |
| 3.5–3.9 | Blue | *A Place Called Freedom* |
| 4.0–4.5 | Purple | *Mrs. Piggle Wiggle* |
| 4.6+ | Black | *Charlotte's Web* |

**FIGURE 7.2.** Karen's color-coding scheme for third grade.

easier than a blue book. Karen is quick to explain that the coding system only begins the process of text–reader matching:

> "After I get the students' reading levels, I meet with them individually and give them an idea of where to start by suggesting two colors. I explain that these levels are 'just right,' but I also tell them that they can try other books if they want to. I remind them that they need to keep up with their reader response journals and have conferences with me. When students know that they will be accountable for what they read, they are a little more careful about making sure that they can read the books."

Karen's colleague Zac uses a similar system but helps students remember their best levels with a desktop reminder that is laminated. (See Figure 7.3 for Zac's desktop reading reminder.) To augment her collection, Karen obtained lists of books appropriate for different grade levels using *The Best Books for Building Literacy for Elementary Students* (Gunning, 2000). This resource is a listing of books at different grade levels by beginning, middle, and end. Labeling books has both advantages and disadvantages; for a discussion of these, see the box on pp. 136–137.

As Karen mentions, she conducts individual conferences with her students once a month. Like other teachers, Karen believes that the best use of her time during the independent reading block is observing and interacting with students (Kelley, 2006; Lee-Daniels & Murray, 2000).

---

Student's Name

My Zone of Proximal Development is

_____ .

The best books for me are these colors _____ .

My reading goal is _____ .

---

**FIGURE 7.3.** Zac's desktop reading level reminder. *This card is laminated and filled in using dry erase markers so that changes can be made as students grow.*

## TO LABEL OR NOT TO LABEL?

Many teachers and library media specialists label the difficulty of books in their collections. They cite both advantages and disadvantages in doing so. These are considerations that teachers and schools should make as they consider labeling books.

### ADVANTAGES OF LABELING BOOKS WITH DIFFICULTY ESTIMATES

Labeling books with difficulty estimates has three distinct advantages. First and foremost, teachers believe that it is especially important for increasing the amount of recreational reading that students do. They note that often students select books based on cover art or topics and then find the text inaccessible. Many readers need assistance with finding books that they can read and understand. Labeling books is *one* scaffold for helping students develop the skill of self-selecting books. Once a reader has an accessible book in his hand, he can then make a choice about the topic and the content, which are also important considerations. Second, many teachers note the importance of guidelines for beginning readers. During self-selected reading first graders chose books above their reading levels over 60% of the time (Donovan et al., 2000). The findings of this study suggested that to gain the important reading practice that they need, beginners need additional assistance in selecting appropriate books. Third, teachers note that labeling is only part of a larger endeavor to perfect text–reader matching. For many teachers difficulty labels are a very prominent scaffold for struggling and inexperienced readers, the importance of which often diminishes as readers become more skilled. Teachers note that monitoring, book talks, discussion with individual readers, lessons on text selection, reader response logs, and assessments also inform readers about their text selections. Together all these supports move readers closer to internalizing their own process for self-selecting books, the ultimate goal of any mechanism for text–reader matching. (See Schirmer & Lockman, 2001, for an excellent article about helping readers develop this metacognitive skill.)

### DISADVANTAGES OF LABELING BOOKS WITH DIFFICULTY ESTIMATES

Labeling books with difficulty estimates can also have disadvantages. The most often noted problem is that the *book* labels become de facto *reader*

*(continued)*

labels. When labeling becomes too prominent or is the only scaffold for helping kids find books, then children can label themselves. For struggling students, labels can be another indicator that they are not up to par and cannot do what the other students can. Second, teachers who successfully use book labels consistently reevaluate their students. When students are not reevaluated, they may continue to read books at a level that is too easy for them. Last, difficulty labels can be over interpreted and inaccurately viewed as representing *the* difficulty of the book as opposed to *an estimate* of the difficulty of the book. Difficulty estimates only approximate difficulty, and readers can handle books at varying levels based on their interest, background, and motivation.

This is the third component of her process. During the self-selected reading time 4 days per week, she meets with one to two students. She and her students talk about the books that they have read, and Karen reviews their reading records. On their reading records, students list the books they have read. During the conference, she also asks them to read out loud two parts from their current book selection. If she notices a number of oral reading errors, she will ask them to rate the difficulty of the book. If the student agrees that the book is too hard, Karen helps to locate a new book.

The final feature of Karen's system is reevaluating reading levels:

"The first year I did this, I didn't reevaluate reading levels in the middle of the year. I discovered that some kids were still hanging onto books that were way too easy at the end of the year. After the summer gap, the students start off slow but by January they have really improved. Many of my kids had never read a chapter book on their own before coming to my classroom. They were so proud and turned on that they didn't want to mess with a good thing. Now, I do stress risking-taking more, especially after they have two or three chapter books under their belts. I also readminister the Classroom Reading Inventory midyear. This gives me a reading level again and helps me to see their progress."

Karen's system makes all the difference in ensuring that her children read daily. The system is not complex or time consuming and does not depend on expensive resources. Without a basic plan for understanding her students' reading levels and the difficulty of the books in her classroom, Karen would not see the growth that she has observed in her students. Many informal reading inventories are available, and most reading specialists can provide teachers with these. Karen's system is very helpful when she acquires new titles or wants to check the difficulty of library books. She does not have to rethink text difficulty every time she encounters a new book.

## CHOOSING NOVELS FOR LITERATURE STUDY: LOOKING AT CLASSWIDE DATA

David is a fifth-grade teacher teaching in an elementary school in a suburb of a major city in the Northeast. At his grade level, the three teachers departmentalize, dividing the responsibilities for the major subject areas between them. David is responsible for teaching three different fifth-grade reading–literature classes. He is very committed to using literature in the classroom and has classroom novel sets to support literature study. In the middle of his third year of teaching, David discovered that the novels he was using varied greatly in difficulty. He explained:

> "I love the literature. Each year we read books like *Holes*; *Thank You, Jackie Robinson*; *Island of the Blue Dolphins*; and *From the Mixed-Up Files of Mrs. Basil E. Frankweiler*. I believe that turning kids on to rich stories is very important. In my class, we read, discuss, keep journals, dress up as characters, make posters and dioramas, and write. Reading good literature motivates the kids and helps in teaching them the literary aspects that are in our state standards. Anyway, I think that I always had an inkling that some of the books were a bit difficult for some of the kids. All of the books that I used were on my district's fifth-grade list, but I wanted to get a feel for how the books compared with each other. I was taking this graduate class and we were looking at different ways to determine readability. Just for the heck of it, I used the Lexile website to look at my novel list."

David looked up the Lexile levels for his novels at the website *www.lexiles.com*. Figure 7.4 shows the Lexile levels for those books as well as the Lexile levels for students. The Lexile range for grade 5 is 750 to 950L. At first glance, the Lexile range for the books was positive. Almost 75% of the titles were appropriate: 33% were at a fifth-grade level and 42% were at a fourth-grade level. So at least 75% of the time, students were reading materials at or below their grade levels. After a closer inspection, David pointed out a few anomalies in the difficulty of the books:

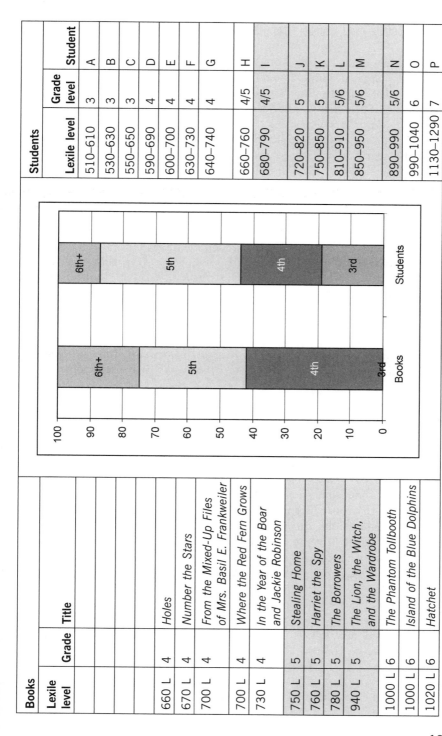

**Books**

| Lexile level | Grade | Title |
|---|---|---|
| | | |
| | | |
| | | |
| 660 L | 4 | Holes |
| 670 L | 4 | Number the Stars |
| 700 L | 4 | From the Mixed-Up Files of Mrs. Basil E. Frankweiler |
| 700 L | 4 | Where the Red Fern Grows |
| 730 L | 4 | In the Year of the Boar and Jackie Robinson |
| 750 L | 5 | Stealing Home |
| 760 L | 5 | Harriet the Spy |
| 780 L | 5 | The Borrowers |
| 940 L | 5 | The Lion, the Witch, and the Wardrobe |
| 1000 L | 6 | The Phantom Tollbooth |
| 1000 L | 6 | Island of the Blue Dolphins |
| 1020 L | 6 | Hatchet |

**Students**

| Lexile level | Grade level | Student |
|---|---|---|
| 510–610 | 3 | A |
| 530–630 | 3 | B |
| 550–650 | 3 | C |
| 590–690 | 4 | D |
| 600–700 | 4 | E |
| 630–730 | 4 | F |
| 640–740 | 4 | G |
| 660–760 | 4/5 | H |
| 680–790 | 4/5 | I |
| 720–820 | 5 | J |
| 750–850 | 5 | K |
| 810–910 | 5/6 | L |
| 850–950 | 5/6 | M |
| 890–990 | 5/6 | N |
| 990–1040 | 6 | O |
| 1130–1290 | 7 | P |

**FIGURE 7.4.** The Lexile levels of David's novels compared with students' Lexile levels.

"Although many of the books fell in the fifth-grade range, I was really surprised about the relative difficulty of several titles. I knew that *Island of the Blue Dolphins* was a tough book but I didn't know that *Hatchet* was as hard or harder. I also didn't consider that *The Borrowers* was as hard as it was. I also realized that I was expecting my students to read some of the hardest books too early in the year."

The book list showed that there was a big gap in text difficulty in David's collection. Many of the books were at the higher end of grade 4 or lower end of grade five (660–780L), but few were at the middle levels of the grade 5 range (850–950L). The leap in difficulty from a book at 780L to a book at 980L meant that students had to shift abruptly from relatively easy books to much harder books over a short time span.

After getting information about text difficulty, David realized that he needed to have a better of understanding of the reading levels of his students. He also realized that this would be more challenging because of the number of students that he taught. Unlike a teacher in a self-contained classroom, David was responsible for the literacy instruction of more than 48 students. In some ways, the departmentalization helped David's teaching to be focused, but in other ways, it made instruction more challenging. Each of his three literacy classes of about 16 students was heterogeneously grouped, so he had a range of ability levels in each class. Knowing that his school gave the Terra Nova in October, David accessed the Lexile levels provided by the test. Figure 7.4 shows students' Lexile levels in one of David's classes. At least 81% of the students were reading at or above the fourth-grade level but 19% were reading at or below the third-grade level. When compared with the levels of the books, the results showed David had done a very good job of paying attention to text–reader matching for the majority of the class. However, 25% of the books, those at or above the sixth-grade level, were not appropriate for most of the class. In fact, the harder books were probably best for only about 13% of the class. The most concerning comparison, however, indicated that 19% of the students were reading at the third-grade level, but none of the materials matched this level. These readers would *never* make progress reading materials a grade level or more above them.

David did not want to give up novel studies, but he knew that something had to change. To solve the problem, David reorganized his novel studies.

"I decided that I simply couldn't have everybody in the class reading the same books all the time. So I added some really easy books to my list to accommodate my lower level readers, but I made sure that the themes and content in the easy titles were interesting and complex. I decided to start the year with a few whole-class studies of the easier novels and then to run two to four novel groups at a time for the remainder of the year. This arrangement allowed students to read materials that were closer to their individual levels. I also added a few more books in the middle ranges of difficulty."

At the beginning of the year, David wanted to model literature discussion. To do so, he took the easier books and asked the class to read them together. This solution ensured that the books were accessible to most students and allowed him to build a foundation for literature discussion and analysis. During most of the year, David set up parallel novel groups based on thematically cohesive books. This way, students were reading materials at their individual reading levels but the class had a unified focus. David used book talks to introduce new titles to students. David kept many of his assignments the same, but the content and the thematic focus were often different. Adding titles meant that he had to keep up with as many as four different novels at a time, but the fact that all three classes were reading the same titles alleviated this stress. As David explained:

"Initially, this plan created more work for me, but once I established a routine, I was amazed at how smoothly it went. Kids started participating in discussions a lot more, probably because they could understand the books better."

Because David increased his understanding of his students and the novels that he was using, he was able to improve text–reader matching.

## COMMUNICATING WITH PARENTS

Rosa currently teaches fourth grade in the Southeast and has done so for 15 years. In addition to fourth grade, she has also taught second and third grades. Rosa noticed that schools often emphasize at-home reading but rarely give parents information and support about how to make at-home reading work. To address the problem, she has designed a handout and a workshop for the parents in her school called "Keeping Them Going: Finding Books for Your Child." In addition, she also provides parents with information about their child's reading level. She explains:

"After several years of teaching I became a little uncomfortable with the confusing messages that we were sending to parents. First, we were telling them to make sure that their children read at least 20 minutes per day at home. However, we were not giving them any information about how to help their children select books and we were not giving them any information about their children's reading levels. Every year it never fails that I send my little flyers home for book orders and I get back orders with titles that I know are too hard for the child for whom they are ordered. Although it's fine to read hard books aloud, this should not be the only at-home reading experience that a child has. I face the same problem around the holiday season and just before summer vacations when parents begin asking me about reading lists. Judging book difficulty is a skill that I have acquired throughout my years of teaching. Because I have read so many children's books and because I know fourth grade, I can usually look at a book myself and know if it will be too difficult for most fourth graders."

Rosa realized that parents needed to find appropriate books for their children to read and that their lack of knowledge about both books and their children's reading levels was standing in the way. Rosa's first step was to inform parents about at-home reading and book difficulty. First, she put together a handout (see Figure 7.5). This handout emphasizes the importance of children practicing reading at home. Rosa noticed that some of her parents were confused about at-home reading:

"In the primary years, parents hear a lot about *reading to* their children but I want them to know that *their child* needs to be doing the reading to get the benefit."

Rosa wanted parents to build reading time into their daily routines as well:

"I tell parents to think about brushing teeth, household chores, and bathing. These are all standard, non-negotiable expectations that they have of their children and reading should be no different. They should help their children find interesting books and then help them to read every night."

Finally, Rosa emphasizes that at-home reading should not be too hard:

"Some parents think that their children should sound like they are working when reading. They don't realize that struggling on every other word actually indicates that the materials are inappropriate and the practice not helpful."

Keeping Them Going: Finding Books for Your Child

1. Readers Read . . . Reading is one of the most important things that your child can do when he/she is not in school. The more practice that your child gets, the better he/she will read.

2. Plan a reading time each day and stick to that time.

3. No more tears . . . At-home practice reading should not be a struggle. Make sure that the books that your child reads are not too hard. We try to check this at school but we need your help too. Children do not benefit from reading books that are too difficult.

4. To judge whether a book is too difficult, follow these steps:
   a. Ask your child to read about half a page or 100 words in a book.
   b. Listen as your child reads and make a tally mark for every word that he/she cannot read or needs help with.
   c. If your child struggles with more than five words per 100, then the book is probably too hard for independent reading.

5. After your child has read a book or section, ask him/her questions about the passage. Reading is not simply pronouncing words. Skilled readers must remember what they have read.

6. To find books to read at the library or bookstore, use the following websites:
   a. *www.gradelevelreadinglists.org*
   b. *www.rif.org*
   c. *www.scholastic.com* (The "kids" button lists titles and also has sample chapters to "try before you buy.")
   d. *www.reading.org* (Click on "Web Resources" and then "Teaching Tools" for a list of children's choices.)

**FIGURE 7.5.** Rosa's handout for parents.

To assist parents in evaluating books, she gives them a simple procedure to use as they listen to their child reading. Rosa tells parents to make a mark for each word that the child struggles. If there are more than five marks per 100 words, then the book is too difficult. In her discussions with parents, Rosa encourages parents to speak up if a book is too hard, and she encourages partnerships.

At the beginning of the year, in conjunction with parent night, Rosa does a 45-minute workshop for parents on at-home reading. During this workshop she has two goals. First, she wants to communicate that at-home reading is a fourth-grade requirement. Second, she wants to support parents in choosing books. To meet the first goal, she explains that students will bring home a book every night and be asked to read this book as part of their homework. Parents are asked to sign off that their child has read. To support parents in choosing books, she presents her handout, gives them lists of books of interest to fourth graders, and then talks about reading levels. Rosa shows parents a number of popular third- and fourth-grade series.

> "I have found fourth graders really like series fiction. Once a student has found a series that he likes, he can find many different books that will immediately be on his reading level. In addition to simplifying the matching process, series help scaffold readers into chapter books because they use the same characters and settings. The reader does not have to continually reacquaint himself with new names and settings."

Rosa uses the workshop time to prepare parents to receive information about their child's estimated reading level. She explains that the school uses assessments to estimate each child's reading level, but she is careful to clarify that the assessments are only *one* piece of information used to find materials.

> "I believe that parents have the right to information about their child's estimated reading level, but I also want them to understand that the assessments just give us a place to start. We expect the reading levels to change and we also expect that the assessments will not be perfect. I tell them that one of the reasons why we need their feedback and support is because the assessments alone will not give us the best picture of the books that their child needs. I am also careful to explain that we expect children to read slightly easier materials when they are reading by themselves. The materials we use for instruction are more challenging."

Because Rosa communicates with parents *before* sending home estimates of reading level, parents understand the information that they are receiving.

Rosa's school uses the Scholastic Reading Inventory, which she judges to be no better or worse than other IRIs. The Scholastic Reading Inventory is a computer-based reading inventory. The assessment uses a modified cloze procedure to estimate the student's reading level. (See Chapter 3 for a description of cloze procedures.) At the beginning of the assessment, the student identifies topics of interest such as sports, dinosaurs, holidays, plants and bugs, and fairytales. The assessment delivers a report with reading levels and a list of books on the student's preferred topics. From Rosa's perspective, the book list feature is particularly helpful:

> "I have had parents take these lists, head straight to the Internet, and buy the titles. They know that the books are ones that their kids can read, and they know that the topics are ones that the child has an expressed interest in."

Essentially, Rosa takes the time to communicate with parents about text–reader matching. She helps them to understand the importance of at-home reading, how to judge the appropriateness of a book, and where to find additional titles. By communicating this important information, Rosa enlists parent support. Rosa explains:

> "The most exciting thing is that I feel like I am educating the parents as well as the students. I am giving the parents important information that they can use even when their child is no longer in my classroom."

## FINDING MATERIALS
## FOR STRUGGLING INTERMEDIATE STUDENTS:
## HIGH-INTEREST/LOW-READABILITY MATERIALS

Cheryl is a Title I reading specialist who also works with struggling fourth-, fifth-, and sixth-grade readers daily in a resource room. Cheryl learned to use text analysis tools when she began stocking her room with interesting materials at appropriate reading levels for her struggling students. She explains:

> "I work with intermediate kids who are often reading on a second-grade level. They come into my room angry about reading and

deeply ashamed of their abilities. What really builds them up, both educationally and emotionally, is reading materials that are interesting and accessible. Kids at this age are observant, and they know what the other kids can do. They desperately want to gain and demonstrate reading prowess but they will not read anything that they perceive to be a 'baby book.' I learned this the hard way. When I began working with this population, I raided the book room for materials at second- and third-grade levels. Unfortunately, this resulted in books with topics that did not interest them or, worse, insulted them. The animal characters seemed babyish, the humor was juvenile, and the themes were too simple. There was a lot of eye rolling. In desperation I started flipping through the catalogs and I finally found high-interest, low-readability materials."

Cheryl made use of readability formulas to help her find appropriate materials for her struggling readers. High-interest, low-readability (high–low) materials contain topics that interest students in the upper grades, but readability levels that match below-grade level performance (Spadorcia, 2005). For high–low materials, authors and publishers attend to the difficulty. Cheryl found that these materials were exactly what she needed to help get her students reading:

"We don't use these kinds of materials exclusively and I don't rely on them instructionally when I can support a small group of readers. But I find that these are really essential when I ask students to read independently or take materials home. They also help at the beginning of the year, when I am still trying to watch kids and figure out exactly what they can do. My students *want* to read these materials and *can* read them and for many of my students that is a new experience."

Cheryl relies on high–low materials most often for independent reading. When she is teaching them directly, she tries to stretch her students and may use materials that are a bit more challenging.

In the Randall and Carol White Reading and Math Center at Oklahoma State, we have found a number of good high–low materials in both narrative and nonfiction genres. Rigby produces a set called *Gigglers*, which are chapter books written at the third-grade level with zany, age-appropriate humor for fourth through sixth graders. Other narrative chapter books include Dominie Press's *Matrix* collection with real-life stories and Modern Curriculum Press's *MCP Early Chapter Books*. Modern Curriculum also has a series targeted for fourth to eighth graders called *MC Comics: The Action Files*, which take the format of a comic book but are written on a 1.5 to 3.5 reading level. The Wright Group's *X-Zone* materials are very popular with older struggling readers in our center. These materials focus on nonfiction topics (e.g., BMX racing, mini creatures) and present the information in a magazine format with photos and stimulating, colorful graphics.

As discussed in Chapter 2, materials adapted to conform to readability formulas can contain other elements that make them difficult. However, high–low books can include unabridged literature. These lower level books have themes that are universal and appeal to many different age groups. In an analysis of 180 high–low materials, Spadorcia (2005) found a large cluster of literature-based books with complex sentences, low decodability, and low counts of high-frequency, but high-coherence, words. Spadorcia (2005), Liang and Aimonette (2004), and Worthy (1996) provide lists of high–low books that are especially motivating to struggling readers. High-interest–low-readability materials fill a gap for struggling readers in the intermediate grades. They are just one of the many applications of text analysis tools.

## IMPORTANT ISSUES IN USING TEXT ANALYSIS TOOLS WITH INTERMEDIATE STUDENTS

Cheryl, Rosa, David, and Karen all used text analysis tools to help them make text–reader matches in the intermediate grades. They worked hard to solve real problems in their classrooms. Although their problems and solutions represent many of the issues that intermediate teachers face, their stories do not represent the entire range of issues in using text analysis tools with intermediate readers. Teachers often want additional information regarding (1) assessment of reading levels, (2) coordinating student reading levels and book levels, and (3) student involvement in evaluating text difficulty.

In order to use text analysis tools, teachers must know their students' reading levels (see the box on pp. 148–149 for ways to estimate a student's reading level). In assessing reading levels, there are additional considerations. First, to the degree possible, one must try to think about the units in which text difficulty will be assessed *before* assessing reading levels. If, for example, one has information about book difficulty in Lexiles or grade levels, then a measure that delivers student levels in the same units will save time. Second, sometimes text analysis tools will over- or underestimate text difficulty (see Chapter 2).

In my work with schools, I have found that teachers may have an estimate of a student reading level in one metric and an estimate of the text difficulty in another. For example, a school might obtain reading

# WAYS TO ESTIMATE
# A STUDENT'S READING LEVEL

One of the most important elements of text–reader matching is establishing a student's reading level. Although this book focuses on text analysis tools, below is a synopsis of four ways to estimate student reading levels. Regardless of the method or the numerical expressions delivered, each method only *approximates* a student's reading level.

## RUNNING RECORD WITH TEXT SAMPLE

To estimate a student's ability to read a particular text, select a 100- to 200-word sample of that text and ask the student to read it orally (Clay, 1993). The difficulty of the text should be known in order to estimate the student's ability to read other materials at or below that level. (See Clay, 1993, for specific marking procedures for running records.) Calculate the percentage of words read correctly. If the student is able to read over 95% or more of the words, then the text is considered to be at an independent level and can be read without assistance (Clay, 1993). If the word accuracy is 94%, then the text is considered to be at an instructional level and should be used when the student has support. If the word accuracy is below 90%, then the text is considered to be frustrational or too difficult with or without support. A running record focuses strictly on word recognition and is the least formal method to estimate reading level. Because they are administered individually, running records may demand more time but they can be frequently readministered.

## INFORMAL READING INVENTORIES

Informal reading inventories (IRIs), as described and listed earlier, are sets of graded paragraphs with accompanying questions. Most have word lists to estimate the best level to begin the assessment. IRIs measure both word recognition skill as well as comprehension of passages at particular grade levels. Most employ readability formulas to establish text difficulty. IRIs deliver independent, instructional, and frustrational reading levels in whole-grade estimates (e.g., 1,2,3). IRIs are administered individually and may take more time. Refer to the additional sidebar in this chapter for a listing of common IRIs.

*(continued)*

## COMPUTER-BASED TESTS

A number of electronic book-matching programs, like Accelerated Reader and Reading Counts, employ computer-based tests to estimate student reading levels. (These programs are discussed at length in the appendix of this book.) These computer-based tests rely on cloze tests. Cloze tests consist of paragraphs with words that have been systematically removed. Test takers must identify the correct words to fill in the blanks from available answer options. Cloze procedures have been used to assess reading levels for some time (Chall & Dale, 1995; Bormuth, 1969). These measures usually deliver a student's independent reading level and an instructional level range in grade and tenths (e.g., 2.3). The difficulty of the passages are determined using readability formulas. Because they are computer based, these assessments are convenient and do not demand a great deal of teacher time. However, they are not more reliable and valid than other methods. In addition, if a student is encountering difficulty with the computer-based format, then results can be invalid.

## STANDARDIZED TESTS

As discussed in Chapter 3, a number of standardized reading assessments estimate reading levels in addition to giving summative information about student performance. Many of the most widely used standardized tests estimate reading levels in Lexiles and deliver a reading level range (e.g., 550L). The advantage of using the reading levels obtained through standardized tests is that the information is already available. The disadvantage is that results might not be immediately available, and frequent reassessment is not an option.

levels of students in grade levels and months but know the difficulty of a textbook in Lexiles. As discussed in Chapter 3, making conversions between systems is not recommended as a regular practice because it will inevitably add more error to the matching process. However, occasional conversions may be necessary. In one case, we used the conversion table in Chapter 3 that translates Lexile ranges into grade levels. We noted that the Lexile range for each grade level was about 200L. The Lexile range for grade 3 is 500 to 700L. So we estimated that books from 500 to 600L were those suited for readers at a level of about 3.0 to 3.4, or the first half of grade 3. Books between 601 and 700L would approximate a 3.5 to 3.9 reading level. When using conversions, teachers need to be even more observant and vigilant about how readers are actually handling texts because conversions introduce more error than is already present in the text difficulty estimates.

An important part of text–reader matching in the intermediate grades is teaching students how to analyze the appropriateness and difficulty of materials themselves. This not only gives them ownership of the task but also equips them for future independent reading in high school and college. In the intermediate grades, metacognitive strategies begin to be important because developmentally students have reached a point at which they can engage in reflective behavior. In comprehension, metacognitive strategies help students analyze and monitor their understandings of text (National Institute of Child Health and Human Development, 2000; Rand Reading Study Group, 2002). One aspect of metacognition, although not widely addressed in the research literature, is judging the difficulty of a text. Schirmer and Lockman (2001) provide an excellent rubric for students to use in evaluating the difficulty of the materials that they are reading. Students read a page of a book and then use the Independent Reading Rubric to judge the difficulty of the book. The rubric is comprehensive and includes 10 factors: vocabulary, sentences, topics and concepts, clarity of ideas, level of abstraction, organization, design and format, genre, interest and motivation, and pacing and fluency. Students must be trained to use this rubric, but the advantage is that it builds metacognitive awareness in areas that will cross over into comprehension strategy instruction. For instance, being able to identify words that one does not understand is the first step in developing vocabulary knowledge. Similarly, analyzing the organization of a text makes students aware of organization.

## SUMMARY

Intermediate readers have usually mastered the foundations of the reading process. In grades 3 through 5, readers understand the alphabetic principle, have acquired a set of words that they access automatically, and can comprehend simple narrative text. They are building fluency and bridging to texts with high vocabulary and content demands. Often in classes like those described, students can appear to be easily reading the provided materials when in reality they are not. If students do not have chances to read engaging, on-level materials, they will not reach the levels of literacy demanded by today's complex society. The vignettes in this chapter show that teachers who make strong text–reader matches in the intermediate grades know how to differentiate their instruction. To quote the International Reading Association's (2000) position statement, they are "making a difference by making it different." These teachers are reflective problem solvers who know that every student must be *actually* reading every day. They integrate available text analysis tools into their practices in ways that match the very principles asserted in the International Reading Association's position statement. They use text analysis tools to build students' desire to read, to increase skills in complex materials, and to involve parents (International Reading Association, 2000). They use text analysis tools to obtain important data, but most importantly they *respond* to the data. When they find that materials are not right, they change their classroom structures, teaching practices, or conversations with parents. They do not allow the text analysis tools to gather dust in their closets but instead put these devices to work in one of the most important instructional activities for intermediate readers.

# APPENDIX

## Applications of Readability Formulas
*Accelerated Reader and Reading Counts*

Although there are many companies and products that apply readability formulas, the electronic book-matching programs, Accelerated Reader (AR) and Reading Counts, are currently the most widely used educational products in the United States. Both of these book-matching programs provide parallel text and reader forms, like those discussed in Chapter 3, but these programs have electronic book quizzes. The quizzing feature makes these programs different from second-generation formulas. After reading books, students take the quizzes and earn points that can be exchanged for prizes or considered in their quarterly grades. I have included this appendix about the electronic book-matching programs because I have found that teachers are hungry for more information. Whenever I conduct workshops about text–reader matching, I almost always have a teacher ask me about AR. Although the professional literature is full of scathing criticisms of these programs, many schools and teachers use them. In my opinion, teachers need basic information about these programs and a clear explanation of what they entail.

When I taught third grade, one of my students, Darius, was somewhat behind in reading but making progress and reading at about a second-grade level. Darius cooperated with reading instruction but when sustained silent reading (SSR) came every day, he engaged in all kinds of diversionary tactics. First, he moved around the room to different reading locations. Then he perused pictures. Sometimes he got chapter books that were too difficult for him and pretended to read them. Sometimes he just put his head down. Other times he whispered and distracted others. As a teacher, what frustrated me the most was that Darius had the potential to read better, and I knew that becoming better would mean reading more. However, Darius read only when he absolutely had to, and I had a hard time motivating him. AR and Reading Counts were designed to motivate students like Darius and help them be accountable for their independent reading. This appendix reviews the basic components of these programs, the available research, and advantages and disadvantages of the programs.

## ACCELERATED READER

AR, created by Judith and Terrance Paul, is a product of Renaissance Learning Systems, a company founded in 1986 as Advantage Learning Systems. According to Renaissance Learning, AR is the most widely used reading program, with more than 65,000 schools using the system. The company describes this program as a computerized system for managing student information (*www. renlearn.com*). STAR Test, another Renaissance Learning Systems product, helps teachers to establish student reading levels. STAR is a computerized test using a modified cloze passage. Books are assigned a difficulty label using the Advantage–TASA Open Standard (ATOS) readability system. To track progress, readers complete computerized AR quizzes and obtain ATOS-assigned points for books based on quiz performance and book difficulty. One of the goals of AR is to motivate readers. The points assigned to readers can be used to track, assess, or reward students depending on how a teacher or school decides to use them.

AR has four components. The first evaluates readers' initial reading levels, the second evaluates texts, the third tests readers' literal recall of books read, and the fourth tracks and reports student knowledge.

To assess students' reading levels initially, AR relies on a cloze test called a STAR assessment (see Chapter 3 for a discussion of cloze procedures). Renaissance has designed two types of STAR cloze tests. The first, called a vocabulary in context, has a single sentence stem. The second, called an authentic text question has an entire paragraph stem. For grades 1–2 each STAR assessment consists of 25 vocabulary-in-context questions and for grades 3 and up the STAR consists of 20 vocabulary-in-context and 5 authentic text questions.

According to Renaissance Learning Systems, the STAR tests can be administered in 10 minutes. There are over 40 reports. The initial information obtained from a STAR test is reported in a STAR Reading Diagnostic Report. The report delivers detailed information about a student. Take for example, the fictitious student, Paige, in third grade. The testing was conducted in March. The report gives us Paige's instructional reading level (IRL) as well as her Zone of Proximal Development (ZPD). This ZPD is Renaissance's term for an independent range. (See Chapter 1 for Vygotsky's notion of the zone of proximal development.) Paige's ZPD is 3.3–4.6, meaning she can independently handle materials between a 3.3 and 4.6 difficulty level as measured by the ATOS formula. Instructionally, Paige can be supported in materials at the fourth-grade level. The STAR test delivers a grade equivalent (GE). Because GEs are often overinterpreted, do not give them too much weight (Schulz & Nicewander, 1997). Paige's GE is 4.4, meaning that she reads at about the same level as other students who have completed the first half of fourth grade. However, her percentile rank, which compares her with other children her own age, is 65. She is performing better than 65% of the students in *her own grade*. This means that at least 35% of students in third grade are scoring better than she is and better than a 4.4 grade equivalency. When measured using the STAR test, Paige is performing slightly above average for a third grader.

Like other companies, Renaissance Learning Systems has its own readability formula. This formula is the ATOS readability formula. This readability formula appears to be a joint effort with Touchstone Applied Science and Associates, Inc. (TASA) [now Questar Assessment], the developer of Degrees of Reading Power. Renaissance Learning scans entire texts of books to obtain text difficulties of AR books, and difficulty is expressed to the nearest tenth of a grade level (i.e., 5.1, 5.2, 5.3). ATOS is a readability formula like those described in Chapters 2 and 3. ATOS uses four features. It assesses word difficulty by estimating the grade levels of words. Words in texts are compared with a rank-ordered list based on *The Educator's Word Frequency Book*, a product of TASA (Zeno et al., 1995) and a listing compiled by Renaissance. ATOS averages word length in syllables (Topping & Paul, 1999). The formula averages the number of words in a sentence. It takes into account the number of words in a book. A company brochure and other publications by Renaissance Learning affiliates mention the Flesch formulas, but the features used are actually evaluated by many other formulas (Renaissance Learning, 2006; Topping & Paul, 1999).

One of the unique features of the AR program is that it assigns point values for performance. The AR quizzes are different from the STAR tests because they do not estimate reading level. They only test knowledge of a particular book. Students earn points for reading books and for correctly answering questions on quizzes. Point values are assigned based on the book's difficulty level and number of words. Quizzes contain 5, 10, or 20 multiple-choice questions. AR offers four types of quizzes: (1) Reading Practice (English, Spanish, and Recorded Voice), (2) Literacy Skills, (3) Textbook Series, and (4) Vocabulary. The more commonly used Reading Practice quizzes contain literal questions. Most of the more than 100,000 quizzes contain simple one-sentence stems, with answer choices consisting of phrases or a single word. Literacy Skills quizzes contain more in-depth questions consisting of a paragraph stem and lengthier answer choices. A student can obtain points based on the percentage of questions answered correctly; no points are received with a score less than 60%. Recorded Voice quizzes provide audio for primary students who may not be able to read but can listen to AR books and take quizzes. Textbook Series quizzes provide questions to accompany specific textbooks.

Based on performance, students can earn points. The points can be used in a number of ways. Some schools use them as reading incentives, allowing students to trade points for prizes in a school store, or as points in grading. Other schools post student's AR points in classrooms or halls, create certificates and awards to recognize students who have earned requisite numbers of points, or have pizza or skating parties for students with certain numbers of points. The AR point values are simply data supplied to teachers based on the difficulty of a text read and the student's performance in answering basic questions. How the points are used (or misused) is up to teachers and schools.

Finally, the AR program provides data to parents, teachers, and administrators, tracking students' progress on quizzes and points. Three common reports are generated through AR: (1) a TOPS report; (2) an AR Diagnostic Report; and (3) a Student Record Report. The TOPS and Student Record Reports provide information on individual students. The AR Diagnostic Report provides information on entire classes.

The TOPS report is usually a take-home report with simple information reporting performance on one quiz and average performance to date. This form contains spaces for teachers and parents to sign. See *www.renlearn.com* for a sample. The AR Diagnostic Report summarizes class performance across a specific timeframe. This is different from the STAR Diagnostic Report that summarizes an *individual student's* reading level. The AR Diagnostic Report lists the number of quizzes passed and taken, book levels, points earned, point goals, and progress toward goals for all the students in a class. Performance is divided by the literal-recall Reading Practice quizzes and the more involved Literacy Skills quizzes. The Student Record Report summarizes individual performance, including a list of books read, performance on quizzes, levels of books read, points earned, and dates of quizzes.

Renaissance Place extends the capabilities of AR by offering an integrated web-based information system. Individuals, schools, or districts can enter data, store them on a central database on the web, and generate reports online. Reports are made available to teachers, district officials, and principals. The advantage of this system is that the data are stored by Renaissance Learning, are available through a number of reports, and can be accessed immediately at any location with web access.

AR is one of the most controversial tools discussed in this book. For this reason, journals and other sources feature commentary and research on AR. To gain an in-depth understanding of AR, teachers should thoroughly research it. AR creators Judith and Terrance Paul and other AR employees or paid consultants have published research and opinion pieces on AR. Clearly, people with ties to Renaissance Learning have a commercial interest in the program, and their work may be biased. In general, opinions and interpretations of AR research run the gamut. Opinion–conceptual pieces as well as primary research on AR are now briefly reviewed.

## Commentary and Opinion on AR

In professional journals and books, researchers, teachers, and librarians voice their opinions about AR or review-related literature (Biggers, 2001; Chenoweth, 2001; Krashen, 2002; Topping & Paul, 1999; Trelease, 2004). These pieces often cite the disadvantages of AR, such as the literal nature of the comprehension questions, the misuses of the point system, and the way that it can narrow the reading curriculum.

The very literal comprehension questions used on AR quizzes may deter readers from thinking about the broader themes in a work. Most of the AR questions require readers to remember facts, like events in a story, details about a setting, or other information expressed explicitly. These questions may lead readers to concentrate on less meaningful details as opposed to broader themes. Furthermore, even if readers are successfully answering literal questions, the AR quizzes do not tell teachers whether readers are thinking deeply and critically about a book. The quizzes may give teachers the false impression that everything is fine when, in fact, a reader may be struggling with higher order thinking. Many commentators disagree with the points system as a basis for motivating readers. They question whether reading will continue once these extrinsic motivators are removed and whether extrinsic motivators send children a message that reading is not intrinsically motivating. They also raise concerns about how AR affects readers at the higher or lower ends of the achievement continuum. Strong, motivated readers probably do not need AR, and readers who are struggling can get discouraged by the competitiveness and public postings of AR points.

Noted read-aloud speaker and expert Jim Trelease (2004) gives an even-handed appraisal of the program in the latest edition of his *Read-Aloud Handbook* (6th edition). He notes that he hears more positive feedback about AR than negative. For instance, he noted that kids read more and spend more time in SSR and libraries report increased circulation. On the downside, he described misguided attempts to use AR points to determine grades, reluctance to run book discussions because the discussions would allow students to "cheat" the quizzing program, and teachers letting AR do their work (see *www.trelease-on-reading.com*; Trelease, 2004). The website has many links to research and other information about AR.

## Research on AR

Actual research conducted on AR falls into three categories: those with positive findings, those with negative findings, and those with mixed findings. Perhaps the most compelling research supporting AR is that cited by the What Works Clearinghouse (*www.whatworks.ed.gov*). This clearinghouse was established in 2002 by the Institute of Education Sciences to provide teachers, schools, and administrators with evidence-based standards on educational interventions. The clearinghouse has specific evidence standards and gives programs grades reflecting if the program had positive, potentially positive, mixed, not discernible, potentially negative, or negative effects on student achievement. Based on a study by Ross, Nunnery, and Goldfeder (2004) involving over 400 students, AR was judged to have potentially positive effects on general reading achievement and comprehension reading achievement. A full description of the report is available at the What Works website. Several studies show positive effects of the program on reading achievement tests (McKnight, 1992; Peak & Dewalt, 1994; Topping & Paul, 1999). Many of these analyses occurred ex post facto. After implementing AR, schools submitted achievement data, which were analyzed. In these studies, gains in test scores occurred when AR was being used. Although we know that gains occurred and that AR was used, we cannot determine that the AR caused these gains because we have no comparison. Better gains may have occurred if a different program or curriculum were in place, or the gains may be attributable to another factor. Some research actually showed mixed results (Pavonetti, Brimmer, & Cipielewski, 2002–2003; Mallette, Henk, & Melnick, 2004; Vollands, Topping, & Evans, 1999). Depending on the study, AR students' attitudes, comprehension, or outside reading was measured. In these studies, AR students did not perform differently than non-AR students or AR resulted in different effects based on gender or school district. In other words, in certain cases, AR showed strong results with some school districts and no results with other school districts. In one study, lower achieving boys showed lower attitudes toward reading (Mallette et al., 2004). Finally, some studies showed outright negative results, with AR students falling behind non-AR students on standardized tests of achievement (Melton et al., 2004). As with many other educational programs, there is no clear consensus regarding AR.

## READING COUNTS

Reading Counts, formerly Electronic Bookshelf, is a product of megapublisher Scholastic. Launched in spring 1999, Reading Counts hit the market at least 10 years after AR. Reading Counts directly competes with the successful AR (Electronic Education Report, 2000). Like AR, Reading Counts extends book matching with a set of computerized quizzes to create student accountability for reading. The program is quite flexible. Initial reading levels can be obtained through Scholastic products or other tests. The program reports text difficulty in three formulas. The major element of the program is a quizzing program.

Reading Counts and AR are somewhat different. First, Reading Counts does not have the history that AR has. Second, it is simpler. The crux of Reading Counts is the computer-based quizzing program. When a school purchases Reading Counts, it is purchasing software with reporting functions, a database listing book difficulty, and quiz packages. Scholastic relies on its other products to complement Reading Counts. For example, Reading Counts does not include an assessment for establishing initial reading levels. The Scholastic Reading Inventory (SRI) can be used to obtain initial reading levels or other assessments. The reports are also straightforward, with fewer pieces of data and more graphics (i.e., bar charts, line graphs).

Reading Counts does not offer a specific Reading Counts measure to assess initial reading levels. Instead, schools can use many different formal and informal assessments to determine a student's level. Reading Counts reports text difficulty in Lexiles, Fountas–Pinnell Guided Reading levels (GRLs), and grade levels. Thus, users can rely on any test that delivers reading level in Lexiles, grade levels, or GRLs. Lexiles can be obtained from a number of standardized reading assessments that are already being used by schools. (See Chapter 3 for a list of some of these.)

Grade levels can be obtained using informal reading inventories. The SRI can also deliver reading levels in Lexiles and grade levels. It offers paper-and-pencil and computerized formats. The SRI is a modified cloze passage. Shorter vocabulary-based items and longer passages form the bulk of the questions. The test takes about 20 minutes. The SRI generates a list of books for the student and a report for the teacher. (For more information on the SRI, see *www.teacher.scholastic.com/products/sri/index.htm*). The Reading Performance Summary reports individual student performance in grade levels and Lexiles. It also gives percentile ranks, normal curve equivalents, and stanines. The SRI reports do not give the test score ranges.

With a Reading Counts package, purchasers receive of database of more than 33,000 titles, with difficulties reported in three formats: (1) grade levels, (2) Lexiles, and (3) GRLs. Because Reading Counts reports text difficulty in multiple formats, schools can use the program in conjunction with whatever system they currently use or prefer.

Reading Counts uses a quizzing system very similar to the AR. The quizzes are computerized, multiple-choice questions based on more than 33,000 titles. Students take these quizzes after reading a title and are then rewarded for performance with points. Questions usually have a simple one-sentence stem and then four answer choices. A unique feature of the quizzing program is that each quiz has a 30-question bank from which actual quiz questions are randomly selected. Therefore, each quiz is unique. Answer choices are also randomly ordered so that students cannot memorize answers. Both of these features prevent cheating. Because each quiz is unique, students can retake them.

At the end of each quiz, students give their opinions about the book using a rating system with an arrow. The pooled opinion data can give the teacher information about which titles are the most popular. Like AR, points are assigned based on book length and student performance. No points are awarded if less than 70% of the questions are answered correctly. After each quiz, the student can receive a personalized report describing books read to date, points earned, number of words read, and dates of quizzes. As with AR, uses (or misuses) of points fall upon teachers and schools.

Like AR, Reading Counts supplies teachers with many different reporting options. The following five are described here: (1) Goals Report; (2) Parent Letter; (3) Reading Progress Update Report; (4) Reading Report Card; and (5) Auto Alerts. The Reading Report Card and the Parent Letter deliver information about individual student progress. The Parent Letter describes the program, number of books read, and points earned by the student as well as the student's goal. The Reading Report Card gives more specific information, including the titles of books read, Lexile levels, grade levels, number of words read, points earned on quizzes, and number of questions answered correctly.

The Reading Progress Update Report summarizes data for an entire class, including quizzes taken, points earned, student reading level, and average quiz score. Like AR, Reading Counts uses certain codes to flag struggling or underperforming students. Auto Alerts pop up when the teacher logs on to Reading Counts and informs her about students who have not taken quizzes recently or who are not performing well. The Goals Report is a bar chart that can be generated for a class, individual, or group. Bars compare actual performance to goals. Other reports give information about point totals; number of books read by a student, class, or group; and pass rates on specific quizzes.

## Research on Reading Counts

Because Reading Counts is so new, there is no research available on it. Several teachers and library media specialists have commented on Reading Counts and its predecessor Electronic Bookshelf (Chenoweth, 2001). However, these papers are not direct research. In general, they critique Reading Counts on the same grounds that they critique AR. The authors note the dependence of quizzes on literal questions, problems with extrinsic rewards, and the limited book titles when these programs are used.

## ADVANTAGES OF AR AND READING COUNTS

AR and Reading Counts would not be so popular if they did not have some advantages (The advantages and disadvantages are summarized in Table A.1.) The first and most obvious advantage of these programs is that they may motivate aliterate students: those who can read but do not want to. Despite strong opposition, extrinsic rewards may jump-start reading for an apathetic crowd. As Jim Trelease points out, adults also reap extrinsic rewards for reading. Professional reading, including research articles, grant proposals, and curriculum manuals, can be unmotivating but grades, grant awards, certificates, diplomas, salaries, royalties, and consulting fees serve as extrinsic motivators. Adults do not always read for purely intrinsic reasons and do respond to extrinsic motivators.

**TABLE A.1. A Summary of the Advantages and Disadvantages of Accelerated Reader (AR) and Reading Counts**

| Advantages | Disadvantages |
|---|---|
| These programs *may motivate apathetic readers who enjoy competition.* | *Extrinsic rewards based on point totals* may lead children to believe that reading has little intrinsic value. Motivation may wane when rewards are removed. |
| The use of Reading Counts or AR can *increase the time and attention that schools give to periods of sustained reading.* | *These packages are not comprehensive reading programs. They are supplemental and should not replace active teaching.* |
| The quizzing component *may help teachers judge whether or not a child has actually read a book.* | These programs rely heavily on *literal questions.* |
| | When overused, these programs *can narrow the curriculum,* squeezing out rich responses to literature like creative interpretations, written responses, and literature circles. |
| | If a school does not have many AR or Reading Counts books, *students may limit themselves to reading only program books.* |

Second, AR and Reading Counts tend to emphasize reading connected texts for uninterrupted periods of time. We know that time spent reading connected text is related to reading achievement (Anderson, Fielding, & Wilson, 1988). Both programs encourage, but do not guarantee, sustained periods of reading. The third advantage of AR and Reading Counts is that the quizzes may be a reliable way to examine whether or not kids are actually reading books. Until these programs were established, there was no method of ensuring that those recreational or free reading books on the list were truly being read. This pragmatic element helps a busy classroom teacher with 30 students to monitor sustained silent reading. Finally, the data management and reporting functions of AR and Reading Counts can make the programs user friendly. As with any computer application, these do require an initial investment of time. However, the programs considerably streamline identifying books for students and tracking progress. The data management elements and parent reports can be helpful in communicating progress in this *one* area.

## DISADVANTAGES OF AR AND READING COUNTS

About six disadvantages of AR and Reading Counts repeatedly emerge in the literature. The first three—use of extrinsic rewards, reliance on AR as total reading program, and focus on literal comprehension—are the most heavily cited. Many teachers, librarians, and researchers question the use of extrinsic rewards like certificates, buttons, candy, stickers, or toys to encourage reading (Biggers, 2001; Carter, 1996; Chenoweth, 2001; Krashen, 2002). They point out that reading should be its own reward and that all these goodies may actually have detrimental long-term effects. Students may receive the wrong message when extrinsic rewards are used: "Reading intrinsically has little reward and so external rewards must be used."

The second major criticism of AR and Reading Counts is that, in some schools, they are implemented as core reading programs as opposed to supplements, as they were intended to be (Carter, 1996; Mallett et al., 2004). When used in this way, teachers do not directly teach and assess students but instead monitor AR and Reading Counts implementation. Children read books of their own choosing and teachers review computerized reports and tally points. They do not teach comprehension strategies, vocabulary, advanced word analysis, or writing. According to Topping and Paul (1999), this is a misuse. AR should only serve as a supplement to a comprehensive reading program with a teacher directly teaching and working with students.

Third, the assessments of text comprehension are extremely literal and cause students to focus on unimportant details as opposed to broad themes and messages. For instance, one AR question for *Tuck Everlasting* by Natalie Babbit asks readers, "When Winnie first met Jesse Tuck she was a) cool and unfriendly; b) disgusted by the boy's manners, c) tongue-tied and awkward, or d) struck by the boy's beauty." The answer is D and, although important, the information is not pivotal. *Tuck Everlasting* is a deep book with many symbols. These literal questions do not really capture its essence. Students who read this book with an eye toward answering quiz questions will miss the depth in the book.

The fourth disadvantage of AR and Reading Counts is that their use can lead to a narrowing of the curriculum. For example, responses to books can become limited to AR quizzes, crowding out creative book talks, dressing as a character, and reporting in first person. Literature circles where more in-depth discussion can take place may be discouraged because students may give away answers to quizzes. Written responses to books and journaling may be replaced by computerized quizzes.

Fifth, these programs may also limit the books that students read. Although more than 23,000 titles have been leveled by AR and 33,000 by Reading Counts, not all schools will have these. These programs may influence text choices in negative ways either by limiting students to specific books or through student strategizing for optimal numbers of points and passing rates. I once worked with a school that had recently adopted AR and was in the initial stages of implementation and asked children to read a specific trade title. Every student that I worked with in one class, regardless of skill, had read this particular title because it was an AR book. For some students, the book was at least two grade levels below their independent reading levels, but they had read it anyway to get points.

## USES OF AR AND READING COUNTS IN THE CLASSROOM

I do not believe that the major purpose of these programs is to consume students with earning points, buying stuff, finding AR books, and taking quizzes. I believe that the major use of programs like AR and Reading Counts is to enhance recreational reading programs so that readers are matched with books that *they can read*. Sometimes called DEAR (Drop Everything and Read) or SSR (sustained silent reading), recreational reading is a time when students read connected texts of their own choosing for specified amounts of time. AR recommends 60 minutes. At least 20 to 30 minutes a day should be devoted to recreational reading. Both AR and Reading Counts have systems to help students locate appropriate books. Many classrooms and entire schools designate a period of time each day during which everyone reads.

Sometimes schools allow these programs to become monsters, taking over their curricula and running the school. Compartmentalizing the program is important. Before opening the door, teachers and administrations should think carefully about how they will implement AR or Reading Counts. For instance, a faculty should discuss how they want to use the point systems. Will the points serve as the primary tool for motivating students? Will points be used for recognition certificates? Will points have purchasing power? Will points be used to qualify for group events like popcorn parties? Will points be ignored altogether?

Schools should compare their classroom and media center offerings with book lists supplied by companies to address several questions: How many of these books do we currently possess? How many books will we need if each child in the building reads only one AR book per week? Two per week? How many books will we need to purchase so that students can regularly participate in this? How will we label the difficulty of books?

Schools should also consider how the use of these programs will change their school media centers and classroom libraries. Will teachers need to share or rotate classroom libraries? Will media centers need to be open more frequently? Schools should consider what purposes the quizzes will serve. The quizzes, if used, should serve as a surface check on whether or not a student has read a book. The quizzes cannot replace discussion and written responses to literature.

Finally, schools need to do some cost analysis. Cost estimates of these programs are not discussed in detail because publishers tend to repackage and reprice items at lightening speed. Accurate estimates are difficult to make. Essentially, the same kind of thought given to buying a new car should be given to buying one of these programs. Like a new car, these programs are not cheap and will probably be with you for some time, so hasty, high-pressure decisions are not advisable.

## SUMMARY

AR and Reading Counts are indeed widely used and quite popular. Like many other packages, they rely on traditional readability formulas to estimate difficulty to match readers with texts. Their contribution, or "selling point," is the quizzing component. This unique element helps teachers check literal comprehension. However, this element should not be overinterpreted. Reports merely deliver information about literal comprehension (and sometimes not well). I believe that these programs can be used appropriately. They are only tools in the hands of professionals. The trick is being proactive and prepared with adequate resources to implement the programs, using some professional judgment, and maintaining limits.

# References

Adams, M. J. (2001). On the Lexile framework. In National Center for Education Statistics (Ed.), *Assessing the Lexile Framework: Results of a panel meeting, NCES 2001–08* (pp. 15–21). Washington, DC: Author.

Allington, R. (1997). Overselling phonics: Five unscientific assertions about reading instruction. *Reading Today, 15*(1), 15.

Allington, R. L. (2001). *What really matters for struggling readers: Designing research-based programs.* New York: Addison Wesley Longman.

Allington, R. (2005, June/July). The other five "pillars" of effective reading instruction. *Reading Today, 22*, 3.

Allington, R., & Woodside-Jiron, H. (1998). Decodable text in beginning reading: Are mandates and policy based on research? *ERS Spectrum, 16*, 3–13.

Anderson, R., Fielding, L., & Wilson, P. (1988). Growth in reading and how children spend their time outside of school. *Reading Research Quarterly, 23*, 285–303.

Atkinson, T. S., Wilhite, K. L., Frey, L. M., & Williams, S. C. (2002). Reading instruction for the struggling reader: Implications for teachers of students with learning disabilities or emotional/behavioral disorders. *Preventing School Failure, 46*(4), 158–162.

Bear, D. R., Invernezzi, M., Templeton, S., & Johnston, F. (2003). *Words their way: Word study for phonics, vocabulary, and spelling instruction* (3rd ed.). Englewood Cliffs, NJ: Prentice-Hall.

Beaver, J. (1997). *Developmental reading assessment.* Upper Saddle River, NJ: Pearson Learning Group.

Beck, I. L. (1997, August/September). Response to "overselling phonics." *Reading Today, 15*, 15.

Beck, I. L., & Block, K.K. (1978). *An analysis of the dimensions that affect the development of code-breaking ability in eight beginning reading programs.* Pittsburgh, PA: University of Pittsburgh, Learning Research and Development Center.

Biancarosa, G., & Snow, C. (2004). *Reading next: A vision for action and research in middle and high school literacy.* Washington, DC: Alliance for Excellence in Education.

Biemiller, A. (2006). Vocabulary development and instruction: A prerequisite for school learning In D. Dickinson & S. Neuman (Eds.), *Handbook of early literacy research* (Vol. 2, pp. 41–51). New York: Guilford Press.

Biggers, D. (2001). The argument against accelerated reader. *Journal of Adolescent and Adult Literacy, 45,* 72–75.

Bloomfield, L., & Barnhart, C. L. (1961). *Let's read: A linguistic approach.* Detroit, MI: Wayne State University Press.

Bormuth, J. R. (1969). *Development of readability analysis.* Washington, DC: Office of Education.

Bormuth, J. R. (1971). *Development of standards of readability: Report of development* (Project No. 9-0237). Chicago: University of Chicago. (ERIC Document Reproduction Service No. ED 054-233).

Brabham, E. G., & Villaume, S. K. (2002). Leveled text: The good news and the bad news. *The Reading Teacher, 55*(5), 438–442.

Brooks, E. J. (1996). *Just-right books for beginning readers: Leveled booklists and strategies.* New York: NY: Scholastic.

Brown, K. (1999). What kind of text—For whom and when? Textual scaffolding for beginning readers. *The Reading Teacher, 53,* 292–307.

California Department of Education (1996). *Guide to California reading initiative of 1996.* Sacramento, CA: Author.

California Department of Education. (1999). *1999–2002 K–8 reading/language arts/ English language development adoption criteria.* Sacramento, CA: Author.

Carroll, J. B., Davies, P., & Richman, B. (1971). *Word frequency book.* Boston: Houghton-Mifflin.

Cartwright, K. B. (in press). *Literary processes and instructional practice.* New York: Guilford Press.

Carver, R. P. (1984). Measuring absolute amounts of reading comprehension using the Rauding Rescaling Procedure. *Journal of Reading Behavior, 17,* 29–53.

Carver, R. P. (1985a). Measuring readability using DRP units. *Journal of Reading Behavior, 17*(4), 303–316.

Carver, R. P. (1985b). Is the Degrees of Reading Power Test valid and reliable? *Journal of Reading, 29*(1), 34–41.

Carver, R. P. (1990). Rescaling the degrees of reading power test to provide valid scores for selecting materials at the instructional level. *Journal of Reading Behavior, 22*(1), 1–18.

Cassidy, J., & Cassidy, D. (2003, December/January). What's hot, what's not for 2003. *Reading Today, 20,* 1.

Caylor, J. S., Sticht, T. G., Fox, L. C., & Ford, P. J. (1973). *Methodologies for determining reading requirements of military occupational specialties* (Tech. Rep. No. 73-5, Human Resources Research Organization). Monterey, CA: HUMRO.

Chall, J. S. (1956). A survey of users of the Dale–Chall formula. *Educational Research Bulletin, 35,* 197–212.

Chall, J. S. (1974). *Readability: An appraisal of research and application.* Essex, UK: Bowker. (Original work published 1967)

Chall, J. S. (1983). *Learning to read: The great debate.* New York: McGraw-Hill. (Original work published 1967)

Chall, J. S. (1984). Readability and prose comprehension: Continuities and discontinuities. In J. Flood (Ed.), *Understanding reading comprehension* (pp. 225–251). Newark, DE: International Reading Association.

Chall, J. S. (1988). The beginning years. In B. L. Zakaluk & S. J. Samuels (Eds.), *Readability: Its past, present and future* (pp. 2–13). Newark, DE: International Reading Association.

Chall, J. S., Bissex, G. L., Conard, S. S., & Harris-Sharples, S. (1996). *Qualitative assessment of text difficulty: A practical guide for teachers and writers.* Brookline, MA: Brookline Books.

Chall, J. S., & Dale, E. (1995). *Readability revisited: The new Dale–Chall readability formula.* Cambridge, MA: Brookline Books.

Chenoweth, K. (2001, September). Keeping score. *School Library Journal, 47,* 48–51.

Clay, M. M. (1985). *The early detection of reading difficulties.* Portsmouth, NH: Heinemann.

Clay, M. M. (1991). Introducing a new storybook to young readers. *The Reading Teacher, 45*(4), 264–273.

Clay, M. M. (1993). *An observation survey of early literacy achievement.* Portsmouth, NH: Heinemann.

Cohen, S. A., & Steinberg, J. E. (1983). Effects of three types of vocabulary on readability of intermediate grade science textbooks: An application of Finn's transfer feature theory. *Reading Research Quarterly, 19,* 86–101.

Cole, A. (1998). Beginner-oriented texts in literature-based classrooms: The segue for a few struggling readers. *The Reading Teacher, 51,* 488–501.

Compton, D. L., Appleton, A. C., & Hosp, M. K. (2004). Exploring the relationship between text-leveling systems and reading accuracy and fluency in second grade students who are average and poor decoders. *Learning Disabilities Research and Practice, 19,* 176–184.

Cunningham, J. W., Spadorcia, S. A., Erickson, K., Koppenhaver, D. A., Sturm, J. M., & Yoder, D. E. (2005). Investigating the instructional supportiveness of leveled texts. *Reading Research Quarterly, 40,* 410–427.

Cunningham, P. M., Hall, D. P., & Defee, M. (1991). Nonability grouped, multilevel instruction: A year in a first grade classroom. *The Reading Teacher, 44,* 566–571.

Dale, E., & Chall, J. S. (1948). *A formula for predicting readability.* Columbus, OH: Ohio State University Bureau of Educational Research. (Reprinted from *Educational Research Bulletin,* 27, 11–20, 37–54)

Daniels, H., Zemelman S., & Bizar, M. (1999). Whole language works: Sixty years of research. *Educational Leadership, 57*(2), 32–37.

Davison, A., & Green, G. (Eds.). (1988). *Critical approaches to readability.* Hillsdale, NJ: Erlbaum.

Davison, A., & Kantor, R. N. (1982). On the failure of readability formulas to define readable text: A case study from adaptations. *Reading Research Quarterly, 17,* 187–209.

Department of the Air Force. (1953). *Guide for Air Force writing: Manual 11-13.* Maxwell, AL: Author.

Donovan, C., Smolkin, L. B., & Lomax, R. G. (2000). Beyond the independent-level text: Considering the reader-text match in first graders' self-selections during Recreational Reading. *Reading Psychology, 21,* 309–333.

Dreyfus, L. (2002, May). *Using the veneer of book levels for emerging and beginning readers*. Paper presented at annual convention of the International Reading Association, San Francisco.

Ehri, L. C. (2005). Learning to read words: Theory, findings, and issues. *Scientific Studies of Reading, 9,* 167–188.

Ehri, L. C., & McCormick, S. (1998). Phases of word learning: Implications for instruction with delayed and disabled readers. *Reading and Writing Quarterly: Overcoming Learning Difficulties, 14,* 135–163.

Electronic Education Report. (2000). *Scholastic learning ventures up focus on Reading Counts! With new position*. Stamford, CT: Simba Information.

Elson, W. H., & Gray, W. S. (1930). *The Elson basic readers, book I and workbook*. Chicago: Scott, Foresman.

Flesch, R. F. (1943). *Marks of a readable style: A study in adult education*. New York: Teachers College Press.

Fletcher, J. M., Francis, D. J., & Foorman, B. (1997, October/November). Only 15–20 percent. *Reading Today, 15,* 18.

Foorman, B. R., Francis, D. J., Davidson, K. C., Harm, M. W., & Griffin, J. (2004). Variability in text feature in six grade 1 basal reading programs. *Scientific Studies of Reading, 8,* 167–219.

Fountas, I., & Pinnell, G. S. (1996). *Guided reading: Good first teaching for all children*. Portsmouth, NH: Heinemann.

Fountas, I., & Pinnell, G. S. (1999). *Matching books to readers. Using leveled books in guided reading, K–3*. Portsmouth, NH: Heinemann.

Fountas, I., & Pinnell, G. S. (2002). *Leveled books for readers, grades 3–6: A companion volume for guiding readers and writers*. Portsmouth, NH: Heinemann.

Fountas, I., & Pinnell, G. S. (2006). *The Fountas and Pinnell leveled book list, K–8 2006–2008 edition*. Portsmouth, NH: Heinemann.

Fresch, M. J. (1995). Self-selected books of beginning readers: Standing before the smorgasbord. In M. Sorensen & B. Lehman (Eds.), *Teaching with children's books: Paths to literature-based instruction* (pp. 121–128). Urbana, IL: National Council of Teachers of English.

Fry, E. B. (1964). A readability estimate for any English language material. *Teacher education*. London: Oxford University Press.

Fry, E. (1969). *The readability graph validated at the primary levels*. Washington, DC: Office of Education.

Fry, E. (1977). Fry's readability graph: Clarification, validity and extension to level 17. *Journal of Reading, 20,* 242–252.

Fry, E. (1980). The new instant word list. *The Reading Teacher, 34*(3), 284–289.

Fry, E. (1989). Readability formulas—Maligned but valid. *Journal of Reading, 32,* 292–297.

Fry, E. (2002). Readability versus leveling. *The Reading Teacher, 56*(3), 286–272.

Gambrell, L. B., Wilson, R. M., & Gantt, W. (1981). Classroom observations of task-attending behaviors of good and poor readers. *Journal of Educational Research, 74,* 400–404.

Gates, A. I. (1926). *A reading vocabulary for the primary grades*. New York: Teachers College, Columbia University.

Gates, A. I., & Russell, D. H. (1938). Types of materials, vocabulary burden, word analysis, and other factors in beginning reading. *The Elementary School Journal, 39,* 27–35.

Gunning, R. (1968). *The technique of clear writing.* New York: McGraw-Hill.

Gunning, T. G. (2000). *Best books for building literacy for elementary school students.* Boston: Allyn & Bacon.

Gunning, T. G. (2002). *Assessing and correcting reading and writing difficulties* (2nd ed.). Boston: Allyn & Bacon.

Gunning, T. G. (2003). The role of readability in today's classrooms. *Top Language Disorders, 23*(3), 175–189.

Guthrie, J., Wighfield, A., Humenick, N. M., Preencevich, K. C., Taboada, A., & Barbarosa, P. (2006). Influences of stimulating tasks on reading motivation and comprehension. *Journal of Educational Research, 99*(3), 232–245.

Hall, S. L., & Moats, L. (1998). *Straight talk about reading: How parents can make a difference during the early years.* Lincolnwood, IL: Contemporary Books.

Harris, A. J., & Jacobson, M. D. (1974). Some comparisons between basic elementary reading vocabularies: Other word lists. *Reading Research Quarterly, 9*(1), 87–109.

Harris. A. J., & Jacobson, M. D. (1978, March). *A framework for reading research.* Paper presented at the annual meeting of the International Reading Association, Houston, TX.

Harris, T. L., & Hodges, R. E. (Eds.). (1995). *The literacy dictionary: The vocabulary of reading and writing.* Newark, DE: International Reading Association.

Harrison, C. (1980). *Readability in the classroom.* Cambridge, UK: Cambridge University Press.

Hart, B., & Risley, T. R. (1995). *Meaningful differences in the everyday experience of young American children.* Baltimore: Brookes.

Hart-Hewins, L., & Wells, J. (1999). *Better books! Better readers: How to choose, use, and level books for children in primary grades.* Portland, ME: Stenhouse.

Hasbrouck, J. E., & Tindal, G. (1992). Curriculum-based oral reading fluency norms in students in grades 2 through 5. *Teaching Exceptional Children, 24,* 41–44.

Hatcher, P. (2000). Predictors of reading recovery book levels. *Journal of Research in Reading, 23*(1), 67–77.

Hicks, C. P., & Villaume, S. K. (2000). Finding our own way: Critical reflections of literacy development of two reading recovery children. *The Reading Teacher, 54,* 398–412.

Hiebert, E. (1998). *Text matters in learning to read* (CIERA Report # 1–001). Ann Arbor, MI: Center for the Improvement of Early Reading Achievement.

Hiebert, E. (2002). Standards, assessments, and text difficulty. In A. E. Farstrup & S. J. Samuels (Eds.), *What research has to say about reading instruction* (pp. 337–369). Newark, DE: International Reading Association.

Hiebert, E. (2005). Word zones for 5,586 most frequent words. Retrieved June 1, 2006, from *http://textproject.org/resources/word-zones-list.*

Hiebert, E., & Fisher, C. W. (2002, April). *Text matters in developing fluent reading.* Paper presented at the annual meeting of the American Educational Research Association, New Orleans.

Hiebert, E., Martin, L., & Menon, S. (2006). Are there alternatives in reading textbooks?: An examination of three beginning reading programs. *Reading and Writing Quarterly, 21*(1), 7–32.

Hiebert, E., & Mesmer, H. A. (2006). Perspectives on the difficulty of beginning reading texts. In D. Dickinson & S. Neuman (Eds.), *Handbook of early literacy* (2nd ed., pp. 395–409). New York: Guilford Press.

Hoffman, J. V. (2002). WORDs (on words in leveled texts for beginning readers). In D. Schallert, C. M. Fairbanks, J. Worthy, B. Maloch, & J. V. Hoffman (Eds.), *51st yearbook of the National Reading Conference* (pp. 59–81). Oak Creek, WI: National Reading Conference.

Hoffman, J. V., Roser, N. L., Salas, R., Patterson, E., & Pennington, J. (2001). Text leveling and "little books" in first grade. *Journal of Literacy Research, 33,* 507–528.

Hoffman, J. V., Sailors, M., & Patterson, J. (2003). *Decodable texts for beginning reading instruction: The year 2000 basals* (CIERA Rep. No. 1-016). Retrieved December 20, 2003, from *http://www.ciera.org/library/reports/*.

International Reading Association. (2000). *Making a difference means making it different: Honoring children's rights to excellent reading instruction.* Newark, DE: Author.

International Reading Association. (2004). *Standards for reading professionals.* Newark, DE: Author.

Irwin, J. W. (1980). The effects of explicitness and clause order on the comprehension of reversible causal relationships. *Reading Research Quarterly, 15,* 477–488.

Jenkins, J., Peyton, J. A., Sanders, E. A., & Vadasy, P. (2004). Effects of decodable texts in supplemental first grade tutoring. *Scientific Studies of Reading, 8,* 53–83.

Jenkins, J., Vadasy, P., Peyton, J. A., & Sanders, E. A. (2003). Decodable text: Where to find it. *The Reading Teacher, 57,* 185–188.

Juel, C. (1988). Learning to read and write: A longitudinal study of 54 children from first through fourth grades. *Journal of Educational Psychology, 80,* 437–447.

Juel, C., & Roper-Schneider, D. (1985). The influence of basal readers on first grade reading. *Reading Research Quarterly, 20,* 134–152.

Kame'enui, E. J., & Simmons, D. C. (1997, October/November). Decodable texts and language of dichotomy: A response to Allington. *Reading Today, 15,* 18.

Kamil, M. (2004). The current state of quantitative research. *Reading Research Quarterly, 39*(1), 100–107.

Kelley, M., & Claussen-Grace, N. (2006). $R^5$: Sustained silent reading makeover that transformed readers. *The Reading Teacher, 60*(2), 148–156.

Kincaid, J. P., Fishburne, R. P., Rogers, R. L., & Chrissom, B. S. (1975). *Derivation of new readability formulas.* Millington, TN: Naval Technical Training Command.

Kitson, H. D. (1921). *The mind of the buyer.* New York: Macmillan.

Klare, G. R. (1954). *Know your reader: The scientific approach to readability.* New York: Hermitage House.

Klare, G. R. (1963). *The measurement of readability.* Ames, IA: University of Iowa Press.

Klare, G. R. (1988). The formative years. In B. L. Zakaluk & S. J. Samuels (Eds.), *Readability: Its past, present, and future* (pp. 14–34). Newark, DE: International Reading Association.

Krashen, S. (2002). Accelerated reader: Does it work? If, so why? *School Libraries in Canada, 22*(2), 24–26, 44.

Lee-Daniels, S. L., & Murray, B. (2000). DEAR me!: What does it take to get children reading? *The Reading Teacher, 54*(2), 154–156.

Lennon, C., & Burdick, H. (2004). *The Lexile Framework as an approach for read-*

*ing measurement and success*. Retrieved June, 2, 2006, from *www.lexile.com/ PDF/Lexile-Reading-Measurement-and-Success-0504.pdf*.

Liang, B. G., & Aimonette, L. (2004). Transitional chapter books. *Book Links, 13*(5), 12–13.

Livey, B. A., & Pressey, S. L. (1923). A method for measuring the "vocabulary burden" of textbooks. *Educational Administration and Supervision, 9*, 389–398.

Mallette, M. H., Henk, W. A., & Melnick, S. A. (2004, Spring). The influence of accelerated reader on the affective literacy orientations of intermediate grade students. *Journal of Literacy Research, 36*(1), 73–84.

McGuffey, J. W. (1836). *McGuffey's eclectic readers*. New York: Wiley.

McKeown, M., & Beck. I. (2003). Taking advantage of read alouds to help children make sense of decontextualized language. In K. van Kleeck, S. Stahl, & E. Bauer (Eds.), *On reading books to children* (pp. 159–176). Mahwah, NJ: Erlbaum.

McKnight, D. (1992). *Using the Accelerated Reader and varied techniques to improve reading attitudes of fifth grade students* (Report no. ED 350582). Fort Lauderdale, FL: NOVA Southeastern University.

Melton, C. M., Smothers, B. C., Anderson, E., Fulton, R., Replogle, W. H., & Thomas, L. (2004, Spring). A study of the effects of accelerated reader program on fifth grade students' reading achievement growth. *Reading Improvement, 41*(1), 18–24.

Menon, S., & Hiebert, E. H. (1999). *Literature anthologies: The task for first-graders*. Ann Arbor, MI: Center for the Improvement of Early Reading Achievement.

Menon, S., & Hiebert, E. H. (2005). A comparison of first graders' reading with little books or literature-based basal anthologies. *Reading Research Quarterly, 40*(1), 12–38.

Mesmer, H. A. (1999). Scaffolding a crucial transition using text with some decodability. *The Reading Teacher, 53*, 130–142.

Mesmer, H. A. (2001a). Examining the theoretical claims about decodable text: Does text decodability lead to greater application of letter/sound knowledge in first grade readers? In J. Hoffman, D. Schalbert, C. Fairbanks, J. Worthy, & B. Maloch (Eds.), *Fiftieth yearbook of the National Reading Conference, 50*, 444–459.

Mesmer, H. A. (2001b). Decodable text: A review of what we know. *Reading Research and Instruction, 40*, 462–483.

Mesmer, H. A. (2004). The art of balancing instructional materials for beginning readers: Becoming a wise consumer. *Balanced Reading Instruction, 10*, 1–11.

Mesmer, H. A. (2005). Decodable text and the first grade reader. *Reading and Writing Quarterly, 2*(1), 61–86.

Mesmer, H. A. (2006). Beginning reading materials: A national survey of primary teachers' reported uses and beliefs. *Journal of Literacy Research, 38*(4), 389–425.

Mesmer, H. A. (2007). *Books for low-income preschoolers: Exploring their quality and lexical reservoirs*. Unpublished manuscript.

Miller, A. (2000). *Book steps: Leveled trade books for guided reading, independent reading, and authentic assessment*. Winnipeg, Manitoba, Canada: Portage & Main Press.

Morris, D. (1983). Concept of word and phoneme awareness in the beginning reader. *Research in the Teaching of English, 17*(4), 359–373.

Morris, D. (1993). The relationship between children's concept of word in text and phoneme awareness in learning to read: A longitudinal study. *Research in the Teaching of English, 27*(2), 133–154.

Morris, D., Bloodgood, J., Lomax, R., & Perney, J. (2003). Developmental steps in learning to read: A longitudinal study in kindergarten and first grade. *Reading Research Quarterly, 38*(3), 302–328.

Muter, V., & Snowling, C. (1998). Concurrent and longitudinal predictors of reading: The role of metalinguistic and short-term memory skills. *Reading Research Quarterly, 33*, 320–337.

Nation, K., & Hulme, C. (1997). Phonemic segmentation, not onset-rime segmentation, predicts early reading and spelling skills. *Reading Research Quarterly, 32*, 154–167.

National Center for Educational Statistics. (2005). *The condition of education.* Washington, DC: Author.

National Institute of Child Health and Human Development. (2000). Report of the National Reading Panel: Teaching children to read: An evidence-based assessment of the scientific research literature on reading and its implications for reading instruction: Reports of the subgroups (NIH Publication No. 00-4754). Jessup, MD: National Institute for Literacy.

Oakland, T., & Lane, H. B. (2004). Language, reading, and readability formulas: Implications for developing and adapting tests. *International Journal of Testing, 4*(3), 239–252.

O'Connor, R. E., Bell, K. M., Harty, K. R., Larkin, L. K., Sackor, S., & Zigmond, N. (2002). Teaching reading to poor readers in the intermediate grades: A comparison of text difficulty. *Journal of Educational Psychology, 94*(3), 474–485.

Oklahoma State Department of Education. (2002). Priority academic student skills. Oklahoma City, OK: Author.

Ozgungor, S., & Guthrie, J. (2004). Interactions among elaborative interrogation, knowledge, and interest in the process of constructing knowledge from text. *Journal of Educational Psychology, 96*(3), 437–443.

Paulson, E. J., & Henry, J. (2002). Does Degrees of Reading Power Assessment reflect the reading process?: An eye-movement examination. *Journal of Adolescent and Adult Literacy, 46*(3), 234–245.

Pavonetti, L. M., Brimmer, K. M., & Cipielewski, J. F. (2002–2003, December/January). Accelerated reader: What are the lasting effects on the reading habits of middle school students exposed to Accelerated Reader in elementary grades? *Journal of Adolescent and Adult Literacy, 46*(4), 300–311.

Peak, J. P., & Dewalt, M. G. (1994). Reading Achievement: Effects of computerized management and enrichment. *ERS Spectrum, 12*(1), 31–35.

Pearson, P. D. (1974). The effects of grammatical complexity on children's comprehension recall, and conception of certain semantic relationships. *Reading Research Quarterly, 10*, 155–192.

Peterson, B. (1988). *Characteristics of texts that support beginning readers.* Unpublished dissertation, Ohio State University.

Peterson, B. (2001). *Literary pathways.* Portsmouth, NH: Heinemann.

Rand Reading Study Group. (2002). *Reading for understanding: Toward an R & D program in reading comprehension.* Jessup, MD: Government Printing Office.

Rashotte, C., & Torgeson, J. K. (1985). Repeated reading and reading fluency in learning disabled children. *Reading Research Quarterly, 20*, 180–188.

Reading Recovery Council of North America. (2004). *Reading Recovery book list 2004*. Worthington, OH: Author.

Renaissance Learning. (2006). *Matching students to books: How to use readability formulas and continuous monitoring to ensure reading success*. Wisconsin Rapids, WI: Author.

Rosenblatt, L. M. (2004). The transactional theory of reading and writing. In R. B. Ruddell & N. J. Unrau (Eds.), *Theoretical models and processes of reading* (5th ed., pp. 1363–1398). Newark, DE: International Reading Association.

Ross, S. M., Nunnery, J., & Goldfeder, E. (2004). *A randomized experiment on the effects of Accelerated Reader/Reading Renaissance in an urban school district: Preliminary evaluation report*. Memphis, TN: University of Memphis, Center for Research in Educational Policy.

Routman, R. (1997). Routman thanks Allington. *Reading Today, 15*(5), 30.

Rumelhart, D. E. (1994). Toward an interactive model of reading. In R. B. Ruddell & H. Singer (Eds.), *Theoretical models and processes of reading* (4th ed., pp. 864–894). Newark, DE: International Reading Association.

Schade, A. (2004). The little read writing book: 20 powerful principles for structure, style, and readability. *Library Journal, 129*(13), 91.

Schirmer, A., & Lockman, B. R. (2001). How do I find a book to read? Middle and high school students use a rubric for self-selecting material for independent reading. *Teaching Exceptional Children, 34*(1), 36–42.

School Publications Branch. (1985). *Reading in junior classes*. Wellington, NZ: Department of Education.

Schulz, E. M., & Nicewander, W. A. (1997). Grade equivalent and IRT representations of growth. *Journal of Educational Measurement, 34*(4), 315–331.

Shymansky, J. A., & Yore, L. D. (1979). Assessing and using readability of elementary science texts. *School Science and Mathematics, 79*, 670–676.

Silvarolli, N. J., & Wheelock, W. H. (2004). *The classroom reading inventory* (10th ed). New York: McGraw-Hill.

Sinnott, J. D. (2002). Postformal thought and adult development. In J. Demick & C. Andreoletti (Eds.), *Handbook of adult development* (pp. 221–238). New York: Plenum Press.

Smith, D., Stenner, A. J., Horabin, I., & Smith, M. (1989). *The Lexile scale in theory and practice: Final report*. Washington, DC: MetaMetrics. (ERIC document reproduction service no. ED 307 577).

Snow, C., Burns, M. S., & Griffin, P. (1998). *Preventing reading difficulties in young children*. Washington, DC: National Academy of Sciences Press.

Spache, G. (1953). A new readability formula for primary-grade reading materials. *The Elementary School Journal, 53*(7), 410–413.

Spache, G. (1972). *Good reading for poor readers* (8th ed.). Champaign, IL: Garrard.

Spadorcia, S. A. (2005). Examining high-interest, low-level books. *Reading and Writing Quarterly, 21*(1), 33–59.

Stahl, S. A., Duffy-Hester, A., & Stahl, K. A. D. (1998). Everything you wanted to know about phonics (but were afraid to ask). *Reading Research Quarterly, 33*, 338–355.

Stanovich, K. (1985). Matthew effects in reading: Some consequences of individual differences in the acquisition of literacy. *Reading Research Quarterly, 21*(4), 360–407.

Stein, M. (1993). *The beginning reading instruction study.* Washington, DC: U.S. Government Printing Office.

Stein, M., Johnson, B., & Gutlohn, L. (1999). Analyzing beginning reading programs: The relationship between decoding instruction and text. *Remedial and Special Education, 20,* 257–287.

Syymusiak, K., & Sibberson, F. (2001). *Beyond leveled books: Supporting transitional grades 2–5.* Portsmouth, ME: Stenhouse.

Taylor, W. L. (1953). Cloze procedure: A new tool for measuring readability. *Journalism Quarterly, 30,* 415–433.

Texas Education Agency. (1997). *1997 Proclamation of the State Board of Education advertising for bids on instructional materials.* Austin, TX: Author.

Texas Education Agency. (2006). *Texas essential knowledge and skills.* Retrieved June 27, 2006, from *www.tea.state.tx.us/teks/index.html.*

Thorndike, E. L. (1921). *A teacher's word book of 10,000 words.* New York: Teachers College, Columbia University.

Topping, K. J., & Paul, T. D. (1999). Computer-assisted assessment of practice at reading: A large scale survey using accelerated reader data. *Reading and Writing Quarterly, 15,* 213–231.

Trelease, J. (2004). *Read-aloud handbook* (6th ed.). New York: Penguin.

Vadasy, P. F., Sanders, E. A., & Peyton, J. A. (2005). Relative effectiveness of reading practice or word-level instruction in supplemental tutoring: How text matters. *Journal of Learning Disabilities, 38,* 364–382.

Venable, G. P. (2003). Readability case study and scenarios. *Topics in Language Disorders, 23*(3), 248–251.

Virginia Department of Education. (2006). Standards of learning. Retrieved June 27, 2006, from *www.pen.k12.va.us/VDOE/Superintendent/Sols/home.shtml.*

Vollands, S. R., Topping, K. J., & Evans, H. M. (1999). Computerized self-assessment of reading comprehension with the Accelerated Reader: Impact on reading achievement and attitude. *Reading and Writing Quarterly, 15*(3), 197–211.

Vygotsky, L. (1978). *Mind in society: The development of higher psychological processes.* Cambridge, MA: Harvard University Press.

Walfish, S., & Watkins, K. M. (2005). Readability level of Health Insurance Portability and Accountability Act notices of privacy practices utilized by academic medical centers. *Evaluation and the Health Professions, 28*(4), 479–486.

Walpole, S., Hayes, T., & Robnolt, V. (1996). Matching second graders to text: The utility of a group-administered comprehension measure. *Reading Research and Instruction, 46*(1), 1–22.

Weaver, B. (2000). *Leveling books, K–6: Matching readers to text.* Newark, DE: International Reading Association.

White, S., & Clements, J. (2001). *Assessing the Lexile Framework: Results of a panel meeting* (Working Paper No. 2001–08). Retrieved from *nces.ed.gov/pubsearch/pubsinfo.asp?pubid=200108.*

Wigfield, A., Guthrie, J. T., Tonks, S., & Perencevich, K. C. (2004). Children's motivation for reading: Domain specificity and instructional influences. *Journal of Educational Research, 97*(6), 299–309.

Woods, M. L. J., & Moe, A. J. (2006). *Analytical reading inventory* (8th ed.). Upper Saddle River, NJ: Prentice-Hall.

Worthy, J. (1996). A matter of interest: Literature that hooks reluctant readers and keeps them reading. *The Reading Teacher, 50*(3), 204–212.

Yore, L., Bisanz, G. L., & Hand, B. (2003). Examining the literacy component of science literacy: 25 years of language arts and science research. *International Journal of Science Education, 25*(6), 689–725.

Zakaluk, B. L., & Samuels, S. J. (1988). *Readability: Its past, present, and future.* Newark, DE: International Reading Association.

Zeno, S. M., Ivens, S. H., Millard, R. T., & Duwuri, R. (1995). *The educator's word frequency guide.* Brewster, NY: Touchstone Applied Science Associates.

Zipf, G. K. (1935). *The psycho-theory of language.* Boston: Houghton Mifflin.

## CHILDREN'S LITERATURE

Adler, D. (1982). *Cam Jansen and the mystery of gold coins.* New York: Dell.

Babbit, N. (1975). *Tuck everlasting.* New York: Farrar, Straus and Giroux.

Banks, L. R. (1982). *The Indian in the cupboard.* New York: Avon.

Berenstain, J., & Berenstain, S. (1997). *Inside, outside, upside down.* New York: Random House Books for Young Readers.

Blume, J. (1976). *Tales of a fourth grade nothing.* New York: Dell Yearling.

Blume, J. (1980). *Superfudge.* New York: Dutton.

Bridwell, N. (1985). *Clifford, the big red dog.* New York: Scholastic.

Brontë, C. (1926). *Jane Eyre.* New York: Macmillan.

Bulla, C. R. (1975). *Shoeshine girl.* New York: Crowell

Bulla, C. R. (1987). *The chalk box kid.* New York: Random House for Young Readers.

Byars, B. (1976). *The TV kid.* New York: Viking Press.

Byars, B. (1994). *The golly sisters go west.* New York: HarperCollins.

Calmenson, S. (1997). *My dog's the best.* New York: Scholastic.

Carson, R. (1962). *Silent spring.* New York: Fawcett Crest

Cervantes, M. S. (1986). *Adventures of Don Quixote.* New York: Farrar, Straus, Giroux.

Clark, A. C. (1968). *2001: A space odyssey.* New York: New American Library.

Cleary, B. (1968). *Ramona.* New York: Morrow.

Cohen, B. (1974). *Thank you, Jackie Robinson.* New York: Lothrop, Lee & Shepard

Cole, J. (1997). *The magic school bus inside the earth.* New York: Scholastic.

Cowley, J. (1986). *Down to town.* Bothell, WA: Wright Group.

Cowley, J. (1986). *Ice cream.* Bothell, WA: Wright Group.

Cowley, J. (1986). *Little brother.* Bothell, WA: Wright Group.

Cowley, J. (1986). *The long, long tail.* Bothell, WA: Wright Group.

Cowley, J. (1987). *I'm bigger than you.* Bothell, WA: Wright Group.

Craig, C. E. (1999). *Moon over Tennessee.* Boston: Houghton Mifflin.

Cutting, J. (1988). *At school.* Bothell, WA: Wright Group.

Cutting, J. (1988). *The barbeque.* Bothell, WA: Wright Group.

Cutting, J. (1988). *Books.* Bothell, WA: Wright Group.

Cutting, J. (1988). *Building blocks.* Bothell, WA: Wright Group.

Cutting, J. (1988). *Faces.* Bothell, WA: Wright Group.

Cutting, J. (1988). *I am.* Bothell, WA: Wright Group.

Cutting, J. (1988). *I get dressed*. Bothell, WA: Wright Group.

Cutting, J. (1988). *I like*. Bothell, WA: Wright Group.

Cutting, J. (1988). *Look at me*. Bothell, WA: Wright Group.

Cutting, J. (1988). *Our grand dad*. Bothell, WA: Wright Group.

Cutting, J. (1988). *What's in this egg?* Bothell, WA: Wright Group.

Dahl, R. (1982). *The BFG*. New York: Farrar, Straus, Giroux.

Davidson, J. W., & Stoff, M. B. (2002). *The American nation*. Englewood Cliffs, NJ: Prentice Hall.

Defoe, D. (1931). *Moll Flanders*. New York: Hogarth.

Defoe, D. (2001). *Robinson Crusoe*. New York: Modern Library.

Depree, H. (1988). *Bubbles*. Bothell, WA: Wright Group.

Dobeck, M. (2002). *Tim's lost fan*. Norman, OK: Saxxon.

Downs, R. B. (1956). *Books that changed the world*. Chicago: American Library Association.

Dr. Seuss. (1960). *Green eggs and ham*. New York: Beginner Books by Random House.

Dr. Seuss. (1985). *The cat in the hat*. New York: Random House Beginner Books.

Eastman, P. D. (1960). *Are you my mother?* New York: Beginner Books by Random House.

Faulkner, W. (1986). *Absalom, Absalom*. New York: Vintage Books.

Fitzhugh, L. (1964). *Harriet the spy*. New York: Dell.

Follett, K. (1995). *A place called freedom*. New York: Crown.

Frank, A. (1953). *Anne Frank: Diary of a young girl*. New York: Pocket Books.

Frost, H., & Jackman, J. (2000). *Cinderella*. Littleton, MA: Sundance.

Gipson, F. (1966). *Old Yeller*. New York: Harper & Row.

Haley, A. (1976). *Roots*. Garden City, NY: Doubleday

Hawthorne, N. (1935). *The scarlet letter*. New York: Heritage Press.

Henkes, K. (1996). *Lilly's purple plastic purse*. New York: Greenwillow.

Hoban, R. (1970). *A bargain for Francis*. New York: Harper & Row.

Hunt, I. (1986). *Across five Aprils*. New York: Berkeley Press.

Juster, N. (1961). *The phantom tollbooth*. New York: Knopf.

Keats, E. J. (1962). *The snowy day*. New York: Viking Press.

Kennedy, J. F. (1961). *Profiles in courage*. New York: Harper.

Konigsburg, E. L. (1996). *From the mixed-up files of Mrs. Basil E. Frankweiler*. Boston: Houghton Mifflin.

Ladd, F. A. (2005). *Scooby-Doo: The ski lesson*. New York: Scholastic Paperbacks.

Lewis, C. S. (1950). *The lion, the witch, and the wardrobe*. New York: Collier Books.

Lewis, P. T. (1971). *Rise of the American nation*. New York: Harcourt Brace Jovanovich.

Lobel, A. (1979). *Frog and Toad are friends*. New York: HarperTrophy.

Lobel, A. (1979). *Frog and Toad together*. New York: HarperTrophy.

Lord, B. (1984). *In the year of the boar and Jackie Robinson*. New York: Harper & Row.

Lowry, L. (1989). *Number the stars*. New York: Bantam Doubleday Dell Books for Young Readers.

Maccarone, G. (1992). *Itchy, itchy chicken pox*. New York: Scholastic.

MacDonald, B. B. (1957). *Mrs. Piggle Wiggle*. Philadelphia: Lippincott.

MacLachan, P. (1985). *Sarah, plain and tall*. New York: Harper & Row.

Marquez, G. G. (1990). *One hundred years of solitude*. New York: Cambridge University Press.

Martin, B. (1989). *Chicka chicka boom boom*. New York: Aladdin.

Martin, B., Jr. (1995). *Brown bear, brown bear, what do you see?* New York: Holt.

Maslen, B. L., & Maslen, J. R. (1987). *Bob books*. Erie, CO: BobBooks.com.

McKee, P. (1966). *Tip and mitten*. Boston: Houghton Mifflin.

Minarik, E. H. (1957). *Little bear*. New York: Harper & Row.

Morris, A. (1993). *Houses and homes*. New York: HarperTrophy.

Morris, A. (2003). *Max, the cat*. New York: McGraw-Hill Reading.

Norton, M. (1953). *The borrowers*. New York: Harcourt, Brace.

O'Dell, S. (1987). *Island of the blue dolphins*. New York: Yearling.

Orwell, G. (1954). *Animal farm*. New York: Harcourt Brace.

Parrish, P. (1992). *Amelia Bedelia*. New York: HarperTrophy.

Paulsen, G. (1996). *Hatchet*. Boston: Houghton Mifflin.

Prince, S. (1999). *Going shopping*. Littleton, MA: Sundance.

Rawls, W. (1961). *Where the red fern grows*. New York: Delacorte.

Robinson, S. (1996). *Stealing home*. New York: HarperCollins.

Rockwell, T. (1973). *How to eat fried worms*. New York: F. Watts.

Rowling, J. K. (1999). *Harry Potter and the sorcerer's stone*. New York: Scholastic.

Royston, A. (1998). *Slinky, scaly snakes!* New York: DK Children.

Rylant, C. (1998). *Poppleton everyday*. New York: Blue Sky Press.

Sachar, L. (1998). *Holes*. New York: Dell Laurel-Leaf Books.

Scieszka, J. (1995). *Math curse*. New York: Viking Press.

Sendak, M. (1963). *Where the wild things are*. New York: Harper & Row.

Shamat, M. W. (1975). *Nate the great*. New York: Dell.

Sobol, D. J. (1963). *Encyclopedia Brown*. New York: T. Nelson.

Spinelli, J. (1992). *Maniac Magee*. New York: HarperCollins.

Thomas, S. M., & Plecase, J. (2002). *Get well, good knight*. New York: Dutton Juvenile.

Thorn, J. T. (1981). *Baseball's greatest games*. New York: Four Winds Press.

de Tocqueville, A. (1954). *Democracy in America*. New York: Vintage Books.

Tolkien, J. R. R. (1997). *The hobbit*. Boston: Houghton Mifflin.

Twain, M. (1965). *The adventures of Tom Sawyer*. New York: Harper & Row.

Warner, G. C. (1977). *Boxcar children*. Chicago: Albert Whitman.

Warner, G. C. (1993). *The boxcar children: Mystery behind the wall*. New York: Scholastic.

White, E. B. (1980). *Charlotte's web*. New York: HarperCollins.

White, E. B. (1999). *Stuart Little*. New York: HarperCollins.

Whitehead, R. (1978). *Ranger Don*. Westchester, IL: Benefic Press.

Wiseman, B. (1991). *Morris the moose*. New York: HarperTrophy.

# Index

"f" following a page number indicates a figure;
"t" following a page number indicates a table.